Antisemitism in Australia

Navigating Hate, Unity, and Policy

Acknowledgments

I extend my deepest gratitude to my family, friends, and colleagues for their unwavering support and encouragement throughout the writing of this book. Your belief in me and my work has been invaluable.

I also wish to acknowledge all those who strive tirelessly for a better society, free from hate and prejudice. Your dedication and efforts inspire hope and drive meaningful change. This book is a testament to your commitment and a call to continue our shared journey towards unity and understanding.

Thank you all.

Hamid Fernana.

Author, Community Leader, Senior Researcher.

Copyright Page

Disclaimer

The information presented in this book, Antisemitism in Australia: Navigating Hate, Unity, and Policy, is derived from open-source materials, including public records, reports, articles, and other publicly accessible documents. The aim of this book is to provide a comprehensive examination of antisemitism in Australia, highlighting its various facets and the intensity of its impact on the Jewish community.

This book is intended to raise awareness, foster understanding, and recommend multifaceted strategies to combat antisemitism, thereby contributing to a more coherent and safe community for all. The opinions expressed herein are those of the author and do not necessarily reflect the views of any affiliated organizations or institutions.

The reader is encouraged to use this book as a resource for further discussion and action against antisemitism, promoting unity and safety within our society. The author assumes no responsibility for any errors or omissions in the information provided and welcomes constructive dialogue and feedback for continuous improvement.

Abstract

'**Antisemitism in Australia: Navigating Hate, Unity, and Policy**' rigorously examines the alarming shift in antisemitism from mere hatred to explicit calls for annihilation. This book exposes the harrowing reality faced by Australia's Jewish community, who are under siege, compelled to move homes and shutter businesses in the face of rising hostility and violent pro-Hamas protests inciting violence with horrifying chants of '**Hunting Jews**' and '**Cull Kike**.' The existential war that Israel wages against relentless adversaries reverberates globally, casting a long shadow over Jews everywhere, including Australia.

In this researched analysis, the urgent need for robust policy and decisive measures becomes unmistakable. Australian authorities and policymakers have danced long enough on the edges of the **Trojan Horse of antisemitism** without effective action. This book argues for immediate, uncompromising intervention to combat the multifaceted threats facing the Jewish community.

Through a combination of legislative fortification, enhanced security measures, comprehensive education programs, and strategic community engagement, this book provides a blueprint for dismantling the structures of hate that endanger Jewish lives and Australian democratic values alike. '**Antisemitism in Australia**' is a clarion call for resolute action, underscoring the dire consequences of inaction and the imperative for a united, robust response to this pervasive threat.

Table of Contents

Introduction

I n the sun-drenched landscapes of Australia, renowned for its laid-back ethos and vibrant multicultural tapestry, a dark shadow has begun to lengthen, casting a pall over the Jewish community. Beneath the Southern Cross, antisemitism, an ancient and insidious hatred, is reemerging with alarming vigor, challenging the very fabric of our diverse society. This book, is a piercing examination of this resurgence, offering a comprehensive analysis of its manifestations, implications, and the urgent need for effective countermeasures.

As we delve deeper into this pressing issue, it becomes clear that combating antisemitism demands a multifaceted approach, addressing the varied and complex challenges posed by this pernicious threat. Each chapter of this book provides an in-depth exploration of different aspects of antisemitism in Australia, shedding light on the lived experiences of the Jewish community and the broader societal impacts.

Chapter One: 'Beneath the Southern Cross: The Complex Faces of Antisemitism in Australia.'

Australia's reputation as a multicultural haven is under siege as antisemitism resurfaces with disturbing intensity. This chapter delves into the resurgence of antisemitism in Australia, highlighting its profound impact on the Jewish community and society at large. It emphasizes the necessity for immediate and concerted efforts, including education, legal reforms, and community involvement, to combat this prejudice. Antisemitic incidents not only threaten physical safety but also have severe psychological effects, particularly on Holocaust survivors and those with affected family histories. Research shows a link between exposure to antisemitic rhetoric and serious health issues, including hypertension, PTSD, and even suicide. The normalization of hate speech further endangers Jewish communities, necessitating comprehensive measures to address and prevent such incidents.

Chapter Two: 'From Hatred to Annihilation: The Global Reality of Antisemitism.'

Antisemitism has metamorphosed into a complex global phenomenon with profound implications. This chapter explores its contemporary forms, focusing on the horrifying attack on Israel on October 7 and its global repercussions. The chapter begins with an analysis of Israel's existential conflict, illustrating how international incidents influence local antisemitic sentiments. It further examines the religious and ideological roots of antisemitism within Islam and the proliferation of radical preachers in Australia, painting a bleak picture of escalating hatred that threatens to annihilate Jewish communities. The necessity for multifaceted strategies to counteract this escalating trend is emphasized, highlighting the roles of education, community engagement, and conflict resolution.

Chapter Three: 'Antisemitism in Limbo: Political Accusations and Academic Controversies.'

The landscape of antisemitism in Australia is marked by a complex state of limbo, where efforts to combat genuine hatred juggle precariously with the preservation of free expression, political critique, and academic freedom. This chapter delves into the intricate dynamics of political and academic discourse surrounding antisemitism. Examining the policies of former Prime Minister Scott Morrison and the political shifts under Anthony Albanese, it highlights the ongoing tensions within Australia's political sphere. The chapter also addresses academic controversies, emphasizing the balance between criticism of Israel and combating antisemitic rhetoric. These debates underscore the precarious state of antisemitism, caught between political accusations and scholarly disputes.

Chapter Four: 'Brothers in Arms: The Jewish Solidarity in Combating Antisemitism.'

The Jewish community's response to antisemitism is marked by strategic and unified approaches encompassing international campaigns, legal advocacy, and grassroots engagement. This chapter highlights efforts by organizations like the World Jewish Congress and the Anti-Defamation League, as well as the Executive Council of Australian Jewry's proactive documentation, legal advocacy, and international collaboration. The roles of Jewish political leaders and the importance of grassroots engagement are emphasized, illustrating the power of unified action in fostering empathy and combating hate. The collective response underscores the necessity of solidarity and strategic collaboration in addressing the spectrum of antisemitic actions and ensuring a safer and more inclusive society.

Chapter Five: 'Legal Safeguards: Policy Measures Against Antisemitism.'

Australia's legislative and policy responses to the resurgence of antisemitism have been woefully inadequate. This chapter argues for a comprehensive overhaul of the legal system to ensure that hate speech and hate crimes are met with the harshest possible penalties. It calls for severe legal consequences, substantial fines, and extended prison sentences as vital deterrents. The chapter also emphasizes the importance of educational programs and awareness campaigns in fostering a culture of empathy and understanding. Enhanced training for law enforcement, stringent oversight of online platforms, and robust community support systems are imperative. This chapter is a demand for unwavering vigilance and decisive measures to eradicate antisemitism from Australian society.

This book is not merely an academic exercise but a clarion call for action. Antisemitism in Australia is not a relic of history but a present danger that threatens the core values of our society. Backed by 20 years of community leadership and 10 years of academic research experience, this analysis lays bare the urgent need for a national reckoning with the deep and complex roots of antisemitism, advocating for a future where hate is confronted, and unity prevails.

Chapter One

Beneath the Southern Cross

The Complex Faces of Antisemitism in Australia

Introduction.

In the sun-drenched landscapes of Australia, renowned for its laid-back ethos and vibrant multicultural tapestry, a shadow has begun to lengthen, casting a pall over the Jewish community. This chapter delves into the disturbing resurgence of antisemitism, a malaise spreading across the nation with renewed vigor. It unpacks the multifaceted manifestations of this deep-seated prejudice, from a sharp uptick in hate crimes catalyzed by significant geopolitical events to the more subtle, yet equally pernicious forms of discrimination that seep into everyday interactions.

The chapter begins by examining the persistence and evolution of antisemitism in Australia. Through the lens of Ben Cohen's concepts of 'Bierkeller' and 'Bistro' antisemitism, and Bari Weiss's 'Purim' and 'Hanukkah' antisemitism, it highlights how these prejudices have been sustained and adapted over time. Testimonies from global leaders and scholars underscore the pervasiveness and adaptability of antisemitic ideologies, which now converge from the ultra-right, ultra-left, and radical Islam. This section emphasizes the need for comprehensive and multifaceted approaches to combating antisemitism, including legislative measures, education, and strong political messaging.

Next, the chapter investigates the alarming rise in overt antisemitic incidents in Australia, presenting a vivid portrayal of a 'Community Under Siege.' It integrates personal narratives, academic scholarship, and journalistic insights to depict the increasing hostility faced by Jewish Australians. This section calls for collective introspection into the roots of this deep-seated animosity and advocates for unity in overcoming these biases through the strength of Australia's diversity.

The exploration of 'Faith and Hate' follows, vividly illustrating how radical rhetoric, often cloaked in religious piety, can undermine communal harmony and provoke significant societal responses. This section paints a troubling picture of escalating religious tensions and societal divisions in Australia. The reactions to these developments underscore the profound challenges facing Australia's multicultural society, and the text calls for stronger legal frameworks and community engagement to address these tensions. Ensuring peace and respect for all members of society is essential not only for the Jewish community but also for maintaining Australia's fabric as a diverse and inclusive nation.

Finally, the chapter examines the impact of pro-Palestinian protests on antisemitism in Australia. This section underscores how the intersection of local protests and global conflicts has notably amplified instances of antisemitism. It highlights the need for stronger legislative measures to address hate speech and incitement effectively, along with enhanced educational efforts to foster understanding and empathy. The chapter concludes with a call for continuous evaluation and adaptation of laws to curb the propagation of hate, ensuring that Australia remains a beacon of multicultural harmony and respect.

Together, these sections reveal how antisemitism is not merely a shadow of history but a stark reality challenging the multicultural ethos of modern Australia, compelling a national confrontation with its deep and complex roots.

1.1 From Marr to Modernity: The Persistence of Antisemitism in Australia.

Throughout history, antisemitism has been a persistent and evolving form of hatred, deeply rooted in cultural, religious, and racial prejudices. Coined by the German journalist Wilhelm Marr in 1879, the term 'antisemitism' was intended to replace the older term 'Judenhass' (hatred of Jews), which was primarily based on religious grounds. Marr's concept extended beyond religious enmity, proposing that Jews were biologically inferior, a theory that has since been discredited. Emil Fackenheim later argued that the spelling should be 'antisemitism' without a hyphen, to avoid implying the existence of an entity called 'Semitism' that could be opposed. This nuanced understanding of the term reflects the multifaceted nature of antisemitism, which has evolved over centuries from religious prejudice to racial and cultural hostility.

In ancient times, Jews faced criticism for their distinct cultural practices. With the rise of Christianity and Islam, theological differences fueled religious antisemitism, painting Jews as the eternal 'other.' By the late 19th century, religious antisemitism gave way to racial antisemitism, epitomized by the Nazi regime's genocidal policies during World War II.

Despite the discrediting of racial antisemitism post-Holocaust, modern antisemitism persists in new guises, such as anti-Zionism and Holocaust denial, which deny Jewish peoplehood and basic rights. These contemporary forms of antisemitism continue to pose significant challenges, necessitating vigilance and comprehensive strategies to combat them.

In the present day, antisemitism is defined by various institutions to encompass its multifaceted nature. The International Holocaust Remembrance Alliance (IHRA) defines antisemitism as a certain perception of Jews that may be expressed as hatred toward them, manifesting in various forms including violent attacks, discrimination, and prejudice. This broad definition highlights that antisemitism is not limited to overt violence but also includes subtle forms of discrimination and dehumanization. The themes commonly found in anti-Jewish rhetoric, ranging from historical myths like Jews as Christ-killers to modern conspiracy theories, illustrate the persistent and pervasive nature of antisemitic ideologies.

Addressing these challenges requires a concerted effort from communities, organizations, and government agencies to recognize, define, and combat antisemitism in all its forms. The active involvement of Jewish organizations, such as the Anti-Defamation Commission, is crucial in ensuring that definitions and strategies are shaped by those who experience the impacts of antisemitism firsthand, thereby preserving the integrity of efforts to combat this enduring form of bigotry.

The persistence and evolution of antisemitism have been extensively documented and analyzed by various scholars and public figures. Ben Cohen's conceptualization of 'Bierkeller' and 'Bistro' antisemitism provides a nuanced understanding of how antisemitic sentiment manifests in both overt and subtle forms. He characterizes 'Bierkeller' antisemitism as blatant and violent, rooted in the direct hatred of Jews, exemplified by Nazi ideology.

In contrast, 'Bistro' antisemitism, according to Cohen, operates under the guise of criticism of Israel, distancing itself from direct antisemitic rhetoric while perpetuating harmful stereotypes and denying the historical continuity of antisemitic violence (Cohen, 2014).

Bari Weiss offers a complementary framework with her distinction between 'Purim' and 'Hanukkah' antisemitism. 'Purim' antisemitism is aligned with the extreme right's genocidal hatred, aiming to physically eliminate Jews. 'Hanukkah' antisemitism, more pervasive and insidious, seeks to marginalize and suppress Jewish identity and support for Israel. Weiss notes that this form of antisemitism pressures Jews to distance themselves from their heritage and align with broader social justice causes, often at the expense of their own community's needs and concerns (Weiss, 2019).

The testimonies of global leaders further underscore the pervasiveness and adaptability of antisemitism. Antonio Guterres, the UN Secretary-General, acknowledges antisemitism as 'the oldest and most permanent form of hatred' (Guterres, 2018). His observation aligns with historical analyses that trace antisemitic sentiments back to ancient prejudices. Similarly, Canadian Prime Minister Justin Trudeau highlights the alarming prevalence of antisemitic hate crimes in Canada, emphasizing the ongoing threat to Jewish communities worldwide (Trudeau, 2023).

Elan Carr, the U.S. Special Envoy to Monitor and Combat Anti-Semitism, points out the convergence of antisemitic ideologies from the ultra-right, ultra-left, and radical Islam, illustrating how disparate groups can unite under the banner of Jew-hatred (Carr, 2019). This convergence is echoed by Ronald S. Lauder, President of the World Jewish Congress, who argues that antisemitism is a universal problem that threatens the fundamental values of liberty and democracy (Lauder, 2019).

The persistence of antisemitic conspiracy theories is a critical component of this phenomenon. Dr. Moshe Kantor, President of the European Jewish Congress, notes that antisemitism is unique among prejudices due to its adherents' belief in Jewish control over society, which feeds into various conspiracy theories (Kantor, 2018). This idea is supported by Gunther Jikeli, who asserts that antisemitic attacks have become more violent and are rooted in deep-seated conspiratorial thinking (Jikeli, 2020).

The academic insights provided by scholars such as David Hirsh and Deborah Lipstadt further elucidate the societal implications of antisemitism. Hirsh argues that antisemitism is an indicator of broader democratic decay, thriving in environments where rational discourse is eroded (Hirsh, 2007). Lipstadt emphasizes that antisemitism and racism are barometers of societal health, warning that societies harboring these prejudices are fundamentally unhealthy and pose a danger to all citizens (Lipstadt, 2024).

Professor Suzanne Rutland's 2023 analysis highlights the alarming rise of antisemitic incidents in Australia, challenging the assumption that antisemitism was a relic of the past. This shift in societal attitudes toward Jews is a cause for concern, as it signals a resurgence of ancient biases in contemporary guise.

In summary, these diverse perspectives highlight the multifaceted nature of contemporary antisemitism. These insights underscore the need for a comprehensive and multifaceted approach to combating antisemitism. This includes legislative measures, education, and strong political messaging to address both the overt and covert manifestations of this age-old hatred. Additionally, fostering interfaith dialogue and promoting cultural understanding are essential to creating a more inclusive and tolerant society. Effective collaboration between government agencies, educational institutions, and community organizations is crucial in this endeavor.

In Australia, recent data by the ECAJ indicates a significant escalation in antisemitic incidents across the country, with a 30% year-on-year increase in reports of verbal abuse, harassment, and intimidation towards Jewish individuals. This alarming trend suggests that antisemites feel increasingly emboldened to act aggressively. Such behavior was particularly evident around synagogues during Jewish holy days and festivals, where verbal abuse and harassment were regularly reported.

Besides several synagogues being vandalized and petrol bombed over the last 30 years, especially in Melbourne, Sydney, Canberra, and Brisbane, this environment of hostility not only threatens the physical safety of Jewish communities but also undermines their ability to practice their faith freely and without fear. The persistence of these violent incidents highlights the urgent need for robust measures to protect Jewish individuals and institutions.

Furthermore, the educational landscape for Jewish students in Australia has become alarmingly hostile, marked by egregious incidents of antisemitic abuse that demand urgent attention. In one harrowing episode on August 6, 2014, around 30 Jewish students, aged 5-12, on a school bus in Sydney's eastern suburbs were subjected to physical and verbal threats. The bus was boarded by a group of teenagers who yelled antisemitic slurs, including 'all Jews must die,' 'kill the Jews,' 'Heil Hitler,' and 'we arere going to slit your throats' at the terrified children.

Similarly, on October 30, 2018, two teenage boys harassed a female Jewish student on a bus, taunting her with remarks like 'What a shame that Hitler didn't kill all the Jews, we would go back and make sure he wipes them all out,' and followed her for two blocks after she exited the bus in eastern Sydney.

In another deeply troubling incident, a public high school student told a Year 7 student that he 'should have died in the gas chambers.' During a modern history class on the Holocaust, a public-school student shouted at a Year 10 Jewish student that 'The Jews deserved it anyway!' Furthermore, students at a private girls' school posed with their arms in the shape of a swastika, took a photo of it, and posted it on Twitter, along with the words 'Burn the Jews,' 'Gas the Jews,' and 'We hate Jews.'

These incidents highlight a disturbing trend of antisemitism in schools, reflecting a broader societal issue that not only endangers Jewish students but also profoundly undermines the principles of safety, respect, and inclusion that educational institutions are meant to uphold.

The alarming increase in antisemitic graffiti incidents further underscores this troubling trend, with reported cases more than doubling in the past year. The content of these graffiti messages is particularly egregious, frequently including calls for the murder of Jews, endorsements of Hitler and Nazism, and Holocaust denial. Notable examples include phrases such as 'Holocaust is a myth,' 'Put them in the oven,' 'no secret that Mossad was behind the Christchurch massacre,' 'Go back to eastern Europe Zionist scum,' and 'We all know Israel was responsible for 9/11.'

These hateful messages not only reflect deep-seated antisemitic beliefs but also contribute to an environment of fear and hostility for Jewish individuals. The proliferation of such graffiti highlights the urgent need for comprehensive strategies to combat antisemitism, including increased surveillance, community education, and strong legal responses.

Such public displays of hatred are not only deeply offensive but also serve to normalize antisemitic rhetoric, potentially inciting further violence. Online platforms have experienced a surge in antisemitic and Nazi sentiment, particularly on far right and white supremacist sites. The propagation of the 'white replacement' theory, which blames Jews for the perceived demise of European races and culture, has significantly contributed to the increase in antisemitic discourse and acts.

For example, an email to a Jewish individual included the words: "When you come across a Jew, strike him in the head, we must fucking wipe them out!" Another email sent to the Jewish Museum read: "Fuck You Jewish we know truth about biggest history lie and we Will fight with truth holocaust never happen." These disturbing trends underscore the critical necessity for proactive and robust measures to counter antisemitism and protect vulnerable communities.

The involvement of far right and white supremacist groups in antisemitic activities is particularly concerning. Subscribers to the 'white replacement' theory, which blames Jews for the perceived demise of European races and culture, often advocate for violence, armed action, revolution, terrorism, and race war, exacerbating the rise in antisemitism. There is growing evidence that individuals who wish to harm Jews are being inspired and reinforced in their views online.

For example, a threat to kill Jews was submitted via contact forms on two Jewish websites, stating: "Me and my friends have already purchased 6 Automatic Rifles as we plan to kill hundreds of Jewish Students on the eve of Purim festivals." These examples illustrate the extreme nature of antisemitic threats and highlight the urgent need for comprehensive strategies to address and combat this rising tide of hate. Enhanced surveillance, community education, and robust legal responses are imperative to curtail the normalization and spread of such dangerous ideologies.

Compounding this threat is the influence of conspiracy theorists like David Icke, who was denied entry to Australia on character grounds but continues to resonate online. His supporters perpetuate anti-Jewish views, linking them to older antisemitic themes and tropes. This underscores the importance of addressing not only overt acts of antisemitism but also the subtle and insidious ways it spreads through conspiracy theories and misinformation.

Additionally, supporters of David Icke have bombarded the Executive Council of Australian Jewry (ECAJ) Co-Chief Executive Officer Peter Wertheim and Research Director Julie Nathan with emails containing antisemitic slurs and threats, highlighting the urgent need for a comprehensive approach to counter the growing recognition of antisemitism in Australia (Nathan, 2019).

The ongoing anti-Israel campaign has also contributed to the rise in antisemitism. Supporters of this campaign often express anti-Jewish hatred online, including on social media pages of anti-Israel and pro-BDS groups. Comments reflecting older antisemitic themes, such as 'Jewish bloodlust' and supposed Jewish control of power, are commonly observed.

This fusion of political and racial hatred complicates efforts to combat antisemitism, as it intertwines legitimate political discourse with prejudiced views. Within Christian and Muslim communities, pockets of antisemitic sentiment persist, often based on theological or political grounds. However, there are encouraging signs of positive engagement through interfaith dialogue and political cooperation, suggesting that community-based efforts can play a crucial role in mitigating antisemitism.

In conclusion, A multifaceted strategy is essential to effectively combat antisemitism and promote social cohesion in Australia. Mainstream recognition of antisemitism within Australian society and the media is crucial for generating the political will to address the issue effectively. Countermeasures should include establishing a national database for hate-motivated crimes, adopting a clear definition of hate crime, and providing education and training for police and other authorities to identify and deal with such crimes.

Jewish community institutions, such as places of worship, schools, and community centers, continue to operate under high-security measures due to the entrenched nature of antisemitism. This necessity, recognized by law enforcement agencies, reflects the ongoing threats against Jews and Jewish communal buildings.

The need for security measures is now extending to other faith communities, indicating a broader deterioration in the social fabric and cohesiveness of Australian society. Government action, such as implementing a Commonwealth law akin to Section 93Z of the NSW law that criminalizes incitement and threats of violence, would be a welcome measure in addressing the persistence of antisemitism in Australia.

The active involvement and advocacy of the Australian Jewish community, including organizations like the Anti-Defamation Commission led by Dr. Dvir Abramovich, are essential in ensuring the effective implementation of these strategies. By allowing Jewish people, as the primary victims of antisemitism, to define it, efforts to combat this enduring form of bigotry can be more targeted and effective, ultimately promoting a more inclusive and cohesive society.

1.2 Community Under Siege: The New Face of Australian Antisemitism.

The October 7 attack by Hamas militants on Israeli communities outside Gaza and the subsequent Israeli response within the coastal strip triggered a significant surge in antisemitic incidents in Australia. According to the Executive Council of Australian Jewry, there were 368 anti-Jewish incidents reported between October 8 and November 19, marking a 41.9% increase from the previous year. These incidents included physical assaults, verbal abuse, harassment, and hate graffiti targeting Jews.

The Australian Jewish community found itself under siege, with many expressing fear and vulnerability. These attacks were not confined to physical assaults but also extended to online harassment and abuse. The accounts of scholars, politicians, journalists, and members of the Jewish community intertwine to present a comprehensive picture of a society grappling with a surge of hatred that has emerged prominently.

The implications of these findings are far-reaching, revealing the pervasive nature of antisemitism. Liberal MP Julian Leeser's testimonies add a human dimension to these statistics. As a Jewish member of the Australian Parliament,

Leeser articulates a reality that many find hard to believe: "We're seeing things that I haven't seen before in my lifetime. Jewish children afraid to wear their uniforms to school, people afraid to wear their Magen David, afraid to wear their kippah."

This statement offers insight into the genuine apprehension that shadows the lives of Jewish Australians, highlighting an environment of fear that has spread throughout the community. This situation marks a societal regression and poses a direct threat to the well-being and security of individuals.

This emerging climate of fear and hostility, underscored by incidents such as Jewish schoolchildren being denied access to play equipment due to their 'Zionist blood money,' as reported by Alex Ryvchin, and the comprehensive data from the Executive Council of Australian Jewry, vividly illustrates the deep infiltration of antisemitism into Australian society. These incidents challenge the narrative of Australia as a bastion of multicultural harmony and tolerance. They underscore the persistence of what historian Robert Wistrich has described as 'the longest hatred,' demonstrating that Australia, despite its ideals, has not been immune to the spread of antisemitism.

This resurgence of prejudice necessitates a critical examination of the underlying causes and a concerted effort to eradicate this malignancy from Australian society. This alarming trend demands a multifaceted response, involving policy initiatives, educational programs, and community outreach, all aimed at combating antisemitism and fostering a culture of understanding and respect across diverse societal segments.

Furthermore, the narrative delves into a particularly disturbing development as it examines the repercussions of rising antisemitism within the realms of culture and creativity. Megan Goldin's 2024 investigation into the plight of Jewish Australian artists unveils a troubling pattern of exclusion and vilification that extends beyond mere social ostracization: "Jewish artists are being pushed by fellow colleagues to denounce Israel as a modern-day Satan or be banished from the local arts scene. They are also deeply wounded by the minimization, justification, and denial by fellow artists of the Oct. 7 murders and rapes".

These individuals, celebrated for their contributions to the rich tapestry of Australian arts, find themselves increasingly marginalized due to a growing insistence on ideological purity. This demand for alignment with specific political or social stances has introduced a toxic element into the artistic community, eroding the foundational principles of creative freedom and expression.

The experiences of Joshua Moshe and Sarah-Jane Feiglin serve as poignant illustrations of the profound impact this environment has had on individual lives. Moshe, a talented saxophonist, became a target for harassment, culminating in his expulsion from a band under the guise of combating antisemitism, an action steeped in irony and contradiction. To rub salt into the wound, Moshe's wife's gift shop has been boycotted and vandalized.

Sarah-Jane Feiglin, an actress, experienced a plight akin to Moshe's, suffering isolation and professional obstacles directly tied to her Jewish identity amid growing antagonism in the arts sector. She expressed the stark reality of her situation, stating, "All of my creative platforms and work opportunities have been taken away from me because I will not be ashamed or apologetic about being Jewish."

This sentiment of exclusion was echoed by Philip Dalidakis, a Jewish former politician, who lamented the seeming impossibility for Jews to advocate for themselves: "Apparently everyone else can lobby on their own behalf except Jews." These experiences underscore a distressing pattern within the artistic community, where Jewish professionals face significant barriers that not only curtail their individual voices but also impede the broader spectrum of creative expression.

The surge of intolerance within the arts community reflects a broader societal issue, where polarization and the radicalization of viewpoints have permeated spaces once celebrated for their inclusivity and diversity. This chilling effect on Jewish creatives, forced to navigate an increasingly antagonistic cultural landscape, highlights the pressing need to confront deep-seated prejudices.

Such exclusionary tactics not only reduce the vibrancy of Australia's cultural scene but also signal a worrying erosion of democratic values and the principles of freedom and tolerance. The experiences of Jewish artists in Australia, as detailed by Goldin, Moshe, Feiglin, and echoed by Dalidakis, necessitate a critical reassessment of the arts communities' roles as inclusive spaces and the urgent need for protective measures against bigotry and hate.

In this context, Dr. Dvir Abramovich, Chairman of the Anti-Defamation Commission in Melbourne, brings to light an alarming trend that exemplifies the extremities of such prejudice. He poignantly asks: "Who would have thought that in 2024, Hitler's evil face would be featured in a leaflet being dropped in people's letter boxes by white supremacists, thereby promoting their genocidal worldview through this well-orchestrated blitz of hate?" Abramovich's observation points to a significant and troubling shift from hidden prejudices to a blatant celebration of hate-filled ideologies, starkly contrasting the country's values.

Further elaborating, Abramovich notes, "There is nothing new about antisemitism in Australia, other than the fact that it has intensified, especially in the wake of October 7," showcasing the incident's fallout as a part of a broader resurgence of antisemitism influenced by various societal factors, including the complexities of inter-community relations. This linkage between the struggles faced by individuals in the cultural sector and the broader dissemination of hate highlights a critical juncture for Australian society, underscoring the interconnectedness of personal experiences with wider ideological movements.

Echoing Abramovich's concerns, Greer Fay Cashman (2024) underscores the escalation in antisemitic incidents, illuminating a pattern of deep-seated discrimination that challenges the core of Australia's multicultural identity. This troubling trend signifies a critical juncture where the ethos of diversity and acceptance paradoxically coexists with ideologies that starkly oppose these values.

Cashman elaborates: "Even before October 7, but certainly with a deeply saddening and gathering momentum since, open antisemitism and virulent hostility towards Israel have surged." She points to alarming statistics monitored by Jewish community organizations, noting a 700% increase in anti-Jewish incidents, predominantly in Melbourne and Sydney, as indicative of a broader issue. This observation leads to the probing question, "When does criticism of Zionism and Israel become anti-Jewish racial hatred?"

Highlighting the underlying issues further, Troy Bramston, in his contributions to The Australian, asserts that the conflict between Israel and Hamas has not only reignited but also exposed layers of old antisemitism, cautioning that "history shows where snowballing hatred can lead." This narrative aligns with Cashman's reflections, shedding light on the nuanced and complex landscape of antisemitism in Australia, where the resurgence of such prejudices poses a stark contradiction to the nation's values of inclusivity and respect.

The observations made by Abramovich and Cashman call for an urgent introspection and response from all facets of Australian society. They highlight the necessity of dissecting and understanding the mechanisms through which such divisive beliefs are propagated, questioning the effectiveness of current approaches to counteract them.

This situation serves as a pivotal moment for Australia, prompting a nationwide reassessment of the principles of inclusivity and respect that should underpin a genuinely multicultural community. It suggests a pressing need for a collaborative effort involving government, civil society, and individual citizens to actively dismantle these harmful narratives, thereby reaffirming Australia's commitment to fostering a society that truly values and upholds the dignity and safety of all its members, regardless of their background or faith.

To fully grasp the depth and persistence of antisemitism in Australia, it is essential to look at its historical roots. Sam Lipski, a seasoned journalist with an illustrious career, offers invaluable insights into the evolution of antisemitism within Australia, providing a historical lens through which the present circumstances can be viewed more clearly. His analysis reveals that the seeds of today's antisemitic climate were sown much earlier than many realize, suggesting a deep-rooted problem within Australian society that extends back several decades. Lipski particularly highlights the anti-Israel demonstrations that occurred during President Chaim Herzog's visit in 1986 as a pivotal moment.

This event, while not as virulent as recent expressions of antisemitism, marked a significant point in the public manifestation of anti-Israel sentiment in Australia, serving as a harbinger for the complex interplay of ideologies that would follow. Lipski stated: "It has been reborn with a vengeance. Like October 7 itself, the penetration of key components in the Australian opinion-making sector, and the sheer hatred which burst to the surface, took Australian Jews and their supporters by surprise."

He further elaborates on the multifaceted nature of this resurgence, observing that. in addition to the hostility, the extremist right-wing antisemitism, which gained momentum during the COVID pandemic by framing it as a Jewish conspiracy, is actively recruiting. However, the greater danger arises from the left intelligentsia. This nuanced perspective adds depth to Lipski's earlier observations, underscoring the contemporary complexities of antisemitism that are intertwined with political ideologies on both ends of the spectrum.

Lipski points out the unique convergence of extremist ideologies from both ends of the political spectrum, creating what he describes as a 'perfect storm' of antisemitism. This situation has placed the Jewish community on constant alert, as the blend of far-right nationalism and radical leftist anti-Zionism has fostered an environment where Jewish Australians frequently encounter hostility. The dynamics of this convergence are complex, involving a mix of geopolitical, social, and historical factors that have intensified antisemitic sentiments, making them more mainstream than ever before.

This toxic atmosphere is exemplified by the personal account of Eliezer, a Jewish Australian businessman, whose experience underscores the real-world consequences of antisemitic rhetoric and actions. Eliezer describes feeling under siege simply for being Jewish, which has necessitated significant alterations to his and others' way of life: "It's not just about feeling unsafe; it's about the palpable need to alter one's daily existence, from business operations to personal interactions, to avoid becoming a target." This shift towards self-preservation reflects a broader societal failure to protect all citizens from hate-based discrimination and violence.

These narratives, both historical and personal, underscore the multifaceted nature of antisemitism in Australia today. They reveal a troubling trend where longstanding prejudices are intersecting with contemporary political and social movements, amplifying the dangers faced by the Jewish community.

The stories of Lipski and Eliezer serve as a stark reminder of the ongoing challenges in combating antisemitism and the importance of understanding its roots to effectively address its manifestations in the present. Through their eyes, we see the critical need for a unified approach that spans across political divides, one that seeks to understand the complex origins of these attitudes and works diligently to create a more inclusive and safe society for everyone.

Amid this turmoil, Jeremy Leibler, the president of the Zionist Federation of Australia, offers a nuanced perspective that highlights the resilience within the Jewish community. He notes a generational shift in the experience of antisemitism, from the shadow of the Holocaust for his parents' generation to a period of relative acceptance for his own, until the recent surge challenged this progress: "Most of my generation never experienced serious antisemitism," Leibler observes, indicating a once-clear generational divide that has been dramatically upended by events like those of October 7, which he describes as erupting 'like a volcano.'

This marked resurgence has not only reintroduced explicit antisemitism into public discourse but has also led to physical and online intimidation, impacting the community's sense of security and livelihood. Despite these challenges, Leibler points to a silver lining: the intensified antisemitism has paradoxically strengthened the Australian Jewish community's identity and connection to Israel, inspiring both significant fundraising efforts for affected families and a wave of solidarity from non-Jewish Australians, many of whom were previously unaware of the depth of antisemitism's impact.

This rallying of support, both locally and internationally, signals a refusal to be cowed by intimidation. Yet, as Leibler's reflections suggest, the question remains: can the cycle of antisemitism be broken, or will it continue to ebb and flow with the geopolitical and social tides?

This section's exploration of antisemitism's resurgence in Australia is underpinned by a nuanced examination of its theoretical foundations, utilizing a social psychological framework to dissect the complex interplay of societal, cultural, and individual factors fueling antisemitic sentiments. Drawing upon theories such as scapegoating, social identity, and in-group vs. out-group dynamics, the discussion extends to a comparative global analysis, situating Australia's experience within the broader spectrum of worldwide patterns.

This approach not only deepens the academic dialogue but also prompts a wider reflection on the psychological, societal, and global forces driving the revival of antisemitism, aiming to illuminate the path toward understanding and combating this prejudice.

In conclusion, integrating personal narratives, academic scholarship, and journalistic insights presents a multifaceted portrayal of the alarming rise of antisemitism, set against

Australia's backdrop of cultural diversity and inclusivity. This contrast spotlights a pivotal societal moment, urging collective introspection into the roots of this deep-seated animosity and exploring avenues for reconciliation and understanding. The concept of a 'Community Under Siege' aptly captures the current climate, where Jewish Australians face increasing hostility.

Highlighting the resilience of those impacted by hate and the concerted efforts to address such biases, the narrative evolves into a compelling argument for action. It emphasizes that overcoming **'The New Face of Australian Antisemitism'** is achievable through unity and leveraging Australia's diversity, aspiring toward a society that upholds tolerance and unity. This analysis not only examines the resurgence of antisemitism but also serves as a call to action for all Australians to foster a future characterized by empathy, respect, and inclusiveness, reflecting the complex faces of antisemitism and the collective resolve to address it.

1.3 Faith and Hate: The Echoes of Radical Rhetoric.

In recent times, Australia has witnessed a concerning rise in antisemitic acts, mirroring a global trend of increased prejudice against Jewish communities. Natasha Frost's investigation sheds light on the breadth of these incidents, from defamatory posters depicting Prime Minister Benjamin Netanyahu to anti-Semitic slogans and Nazi salutes at pro-Palestinian gatherings outside the Jewish Museum.

These acts not only indicate escalating religious tensions but also deepen societal rifts, exemplified by the departure of several Australian rabbis from the Jewish Muslim Christian Association. This exodus highlights a breakdown in interfaith dialogue, attributed to some religious leaders' failure to denounce the violence in Israel, further marginalizing the Jewish community and intensifying feelings of isolation and vulnerability.

Despite strides made by many Christian institutions in Australia towards reconciliation and respect for Judaism, pockets of hostility towards Jews and Judaism persist among certain churches and religious leaders. While overt expressions of antisemitism are less common among mainstream Australian Christians compared to counterparts in Europe and the Americas, instances where comments from clerical figures could be deemed antisemitic according to the IHRA Working Definition have occurred. Pope Francis has strongly condemned antisemitism, emphasizing that it contradicts Christian beliefs and represents a rejection of one's own origins.

Christianity and its leaders in Australia have faced criticism for perpetuating antisemitic attitudes and behaviors. Several incidents involving public statements by Christian figures have been perceived as antisemitic. For example, a priest's comment in a major tabloid that 'Zionists' are promoting a showdown between Judeo-Christianity and Islam was seen as promoting a harmful narrative targeting Jews. Additionally, certain Christian groups in Australia have propagated conspiracy theories and antisemitic ideologies, contributing to a climate of fear and hostility towards Jews.

Despite these challenges, some Christian leaders in Australia have spoken out against antisemitism and condemned the persecution of Jews. For instance, the Catholic Church in Australia has publicly disavowed antisemitism and declared it a sin. The Uniting Church in Australia has also engaged in dialogue with the Jewish community and reviewed its theology to improve relations with other faiths and Christian streams. While some Christian figures have expressed hateful views towards Judaism and Jews, many others have worked to promote understanding and tolerance between different faith communities.

Notably, Bishop George Browning, former Anglican bishop of Canberra and Goulburn and President of the Australia Palestine Advocacy Network (APAN), has been a prominent figure in the discourse on the Israel-Palestinian conflict. However, some of Browning's articles have been criticized for meeting certain criteria of the IHRA Working Definition of Anti-Semitism. In one instance, Browning accused the Executive Council of Australian Jewry (ECAJ) of influencing the Australian government to cancel a Palestinian's visa, a claim for which there was no evidence. Browning's inaccurate description of Israel's Nation-State law was also viewed as inflammatory. These incidents highlight the complexities of addressing antisemitism within the Australian Christian community.

Father Rod Bower of the Anglican Parish of Gosford has also been involved in controversies regarding his statements on the treatment of refugees and asylum seekers. His comparison of the situation on Manus Island to the early stages of the Holocaust sparked debate and criticism, with some viewing his comments as inappropriate. Despite apologizing for causing offense, Bower's remarks remained a point of contention, illustrating the challenges of addressing sensitive historical narratives within contemporary discourse.

In response to Bower's comments, Vic Alhadeff, CEO of the NSW Jewish Board of Deputies, emphasized the importance of avoiding comparisons between contemporary issues and the Holocaust. Alhadeff argued that such analogies are irresponsible and hurtful to Holocaust survivors and their families. These incidents underscore the need for nuanced and respectful dialogue to address antisemitism and promote understanding among diverse religious communities in Australia.

Shifting focus from Christian antisemitism to its manifestations within Islamic contexts, it is essential to acknowledge the diversity within Muslim communities in Australia, which encompass a range of religious, ethnic, and political backgrounds. While there are effective interfaith programs and dialogues between Muslims and Jews aimed at fostering mutual understanding, there are also individuals and groups within the Muslim community who express and promote anti-Jewish views, sometimes mixing religious and political motives. It's important to note that these views may not necessarily represent authentic Islamic beliefs.

El-Telegraph, a Melbourne-based Arabic newspaper that claims to be the largest and longest-running Arabic newspaper in Australia, publishes several highly antisemitic articles read by both Christians and Muslims. Contributing author Pierre Semaan promotes antisemitic conspiracy theories, including claims that the Rothschild family controls the world's wealth, governments, and militaries. He suggests that tensions and wars in several countries are orchestrated by the Rothschilds to expand their control, particularly through Jewish immigration to Israel. Semaan also implies that Israel's actions are part of a plan to bring about the arrival of the Jewish Messiah.

Al Quds - Melbourne, a pro-Iranian Shiite group, and Hizb ut-Tahrir (HT), an organization campaigning for a global caliphate, pose significant threats to Australian Jewish communities through their persistent antisemitic rhetoric. Al Quds - Melbourne frequently calls for the annihilation of Israel and publishes dehumanizing and demonizing allegations about Jews on their Facebook page, aligning with the IHRA Working Definition of Antisemitism. Similarly, HT opposes Israel's existence and shares content on social media that makes dehumanizing allegations about Jews, including false claims about Jewish involvement in World War II and the Holocaust, furthering antisemitic sentiments.

In this climate of escalating communal tensions, on December 22, 3, Imam Ahmad Zoud delivered a sermon filled with antisemitic rhetoric at the Masjid as-Sunnah Lakemba in Sydney, labeling Jews as "bloodthirsty, treacherous monsters" and mocking the victims of the October 7 Hamas attacks. He depicted Jews as inherently violent, asserting that they raise their children with principles of violence, terrorism, and killing. Later, in a subsequent sermon on February 9, Zoud characterized Jews as "criminal, barbaric, tyrannical," and advocated for Jihad as the sole solution to conflicts, categorically rejecting peaceful resolutions. This highlights a disturbing trend of hate speech veiled as religious discourse (Milionis, 2024).

These sermons have ignited considerable backlash. Liberal Senator Dave Sharma and David Ossip from the NSW Jewish Board of Deputies sharply criticized Zoud's statements. Sharma suggested that such speech, if not already illegal, should be, denouncing it as an incitement to violence. Ossip underscored the dangerous nature of such rhetoric, stating it was "incredibly dangerous" and "inconsistent with Australian values." Both leaders emphasized the critical need to maintain communal cohesion and to staunchly oppose violence-inciting hate speech.

Additionally, Sky News host Andrew Bolt highlighted the concerning trends within the Australian political landscape, which he argued have compromised community safety and stoked fears among Jewish Australians. Reporting on another related incident, James Morrow noted the widespread condemnation from both political sides against Brother Ismail, a preacher who lauded Hamas' actions as heroic and called for jihad.

This rhetoric was part of content from the Al Madina Dawah Centre, which included videos on YouTube that propagated antisemitic messages, describing Jews as deceitful and controlling major financial systems. Abu Ousayd, another preacher from the same center, has also delivered sermons filled with harmful stereotypes and incitation, referencing Islamic scriptures that call for violence against Jews, labeling them as "descendants of pigs and monkeys," a deeply offensive antisemitic trope.

In response to the hate-fueled sermons by Islamic clerics, political figures like Opposition home affairs spokesman James Paterson have advocated for the deportation of non-citizen preachers who incite hatred. Education Minister Jason Clare and Workplace Minister Tony Burke have strongly condemned these antisemitic remarks, asserting that there is no place for such hate in Australia. State member for Bankstown, Jihad Dib, emphasized the importance of interfaith and intercultural dialogue during these tumultuous times, declaring both antisemitism and Islamophobia unacceptable in Australia's multicultural society.

The incidents and the reactions they provoked underscore the troubling pattern of radical rhetoric masquerading as religious guidance, as highlighted by Peta Credlin on Sky News: "This situation demonstrates how deep-seated prejudices can disrupt interreligious harmony and suggests a need for stronger enforcement of anti-racism laws to maintain communal peace and uphold Australian values."

The Executive Council of Australian Jewry (ECAJ) has responded by formally lodging a vilification complaint with the Human Rights Commission against the implicated Islamic preachers, as detailed by Ellen Ransley. The ECAJ, led by deputy president Robert Goot SC, aims to protect the Jewish community's honor, and safeguard the future fabric of Australian society. The council is outraged by the sermons' content and is exploring all legal options.

ECAJ president Daniel Aghion stressed the need for urgent legal reform to combat hate speech and foster a peaceful, cohesive society, advocating for legal action to protect not only the Jewish community but all Australians from racist behavior. Federal minister Tony Burke has also expressed support for stronger legal actions against such hate speech, underscoring the necessity of a robust legal framework to address these challenges effectively.

In another particularly alarming incident, pro-Palestinian activists Laura Allam and Mohammad Sharab face charges related to the alleged kidnapping and assault of a man in Melbourne, an attack purportedly motivated by the victim's employment with a Jewish individual. The details of the case emerged following the lifting of a suppression order in the Melbourne Magistrates' Court, revealing a harrowing ordeal where the victim was lured into an ambush, assaulted with a hammer, and suffered severe physical abuse.

Kristian Silva, a court reporter, highlighted that the attack led to significant injuries for the victim, including fractures and cuts. Allam, a human rights activist and founder of the Al Jannah Foundation, alongside Sharab, allegedly coordinated this violent act, which police initially suggested was not motivated by racial or political issues despite the victim and Allam's shared history in political activism related to the Israel-Gaza conflict.

Furthermore, Allam, who has been released on bail, has drawn public attention due to his work with the Al Jannah Foundation, which aims to support Palestinian families affected by conflict and facilitate their resettlement in Australia. The lifting of the suppression order allows for a wider public discourse on the incident, set against the backdrop of the Israel-Gaza conflict and the activists' involvement in related political activities. The case's progression through the legal system will likely continue to attract media coverage, especially as it touches on sensitive themes of race, politics, and the complexities of activism.

Similarly, Dr. Jamal Rifi, a Lebanese-born Muslim community leader in Sydney, faced harassment and threats for his involvement with Project Rozana, a charity that supports medical treatment for Palestinian children in Israeli hospitals. The charity was founded by a Jewish organization, Hadassah Australia, leading to accusations against Dr. Rifi of 'working for the Zionists.' This case highlights antisemitism by association, where individuals face hostility for their perceived support of Jewish causes, even if they are not Jewish themselves.

In conclusion, the exploration of '**Faith and Hate**' vividly illustrates how radical rhetoric, often cloaked in religious piety, can undermine communal harmony and provoke significant societal responses. This exposes the intensification of antisemitic acts and rhetoric in Australia, painting a troubling picture of escalating religious tensions and societal divisions. The reactions to these developments, from community responses to legal actions, underscore the profound challenges facing Australia's multicultural society. Moving forward, it becomes imperative to address these tensions through stronger legal frameworks and community engagement, ensuring that all members of society can live together in peace and respect, free from fear and discrimination. This resolution is critical not only for the Jewish community but for maintaining Australia's fabric as a diverse and inclusive nation.

1.4 From Streets to Sentiments: The Impact of Pro-Palestinian Protests on Antisemitism in Australia.

In the aftermath of the October 7 attacks, Australia has witnessed a significant escalation in pro-Palestinian protests, characterized not only by their increased frequency and intensity but also by their composition: a diverse amalgamation of participants that includes Muslim communities, white supremacists, academics, and students. This eclectic mix of protesters, united under the pro-Palestinian banner, has led to a marked increase in violent demonstrations, profoundly impacting the nation's social fabric.

The intensity and breadth of these protests have particularly resonated in Melbourne's northern suburbs, where the heightened tensions and sporadic outbreaks of violence have unsettled the local Jewish community. Concerns over personal safety and the security of their properties have compelled many Jewish business owners to relocate their families and businesses, seeking refuge in safer areas.

This movement has not only altered the demographic and economic atmosphere of these suburbs but has also underscored the deep divisions and escalating animosities that these protests have engendered within Australian society, challenging the multicultural harmony that the nation has long endeavored to maintain.

Amidst this charged atmosphere, on November 11, 2023, a significant protest at Sydney's Port Botany escalated the tension. Hundreds of pro-Palestinian demonstrators successfully prevented the docking of the Israeli cargo ship Contship Dax, operated by ZIM. This protest was part of a broader campaign aimed at economically targeting Israeli interests, illustrating the global scale and local impact of such movements.

Paddy Gibson of Trade Unionists for Palestine emphasized the strategy to economically weaken Israel by disrupting its shipping operations worldwide. He was quoted by the broadcaster as saying, "They're in every port of the world, which means we can fight them in every port of the world and bring them to their knees," and added, "Start hitting them economically where it hurts." (TRT World).

Similarly, Briana Charles reports for Al-Jazeera on January 29, 2024, about the ongoing pro-Palestinian protests in Australia, particularly focusing on the disruption at Melbourne ports. Activists have targeted Israeli ships, notably the ZIM Ganges, leading to several days of blockade at the Port of Melbourne. The protest, which saw the police using pepper spray to disperse demonstrators, resulted in dozens of arrests and the temporary closure of the Victorian International Container Terminal (VICT).

Among the protesters was Tasnim Mahmoud Sammak from Free Palestine Melbourne, who highlighted her personal connection to the crisis in Gaza. Also present was Melbourne-based Palestinian artist Sofia Sabbagh, who described the police formation as intimidating, leading to confrontations where protestors, including Sabbagh, were pushed away from their supplies and one individual was forcibly removed from a wheelchair.

Victoria Police defended their actions by citing the need to manage the dynamic and potentially aggressive situation at the blockade. In response to anticipated disruptions from pro-Palestine protests in Melbourne's CBD, aimed at causing 'economic pain' due to Israel's military actions in Gaza, Victoria Police are redeploying hundreds of officers from regional stations. The protest group A15 Action has promised to target major economic points such as the Port of Melbourne, train stations, and company offices linked to Israel.

The protests are part of a global movement intending to disrupt key transport hubs and business centers in at least 30 cities worldwide. During recent events, police arrested ten demonstrators at the Port of Melbourne after clashes. This protest activity aligns with a broader campaign to express solidarity with Palestinians, following significant casualties in the ongoing conflict between Israel and Hamas (C. Houston & A. McMillan, 2024).

Further complicating the discourse, another protest in Melbourne led to a confrontation at a hotel where an Israeli delegation was staying, highlighting the intense personal and diplomatic stakes involved. The delegation, which included relatives of Israelis affected by Hamas actions, was subjected to aggressive protests that disrupted their engagements.

This incident drew sharp rebukes from figures like Victoria state premier Jacinta Allan and Prime Minister Anthony Albanese, who condemned the protesters' actions as detrimental to peace efforts and inappropriate given the circumstances. Such events not only reflect the direct impact of global conflicts on local communities but also challenge

Australia's multicultural ethos and its commitment to maintaining social cohesion amid diverging global allegiances (P. Mercer, 2023).

This incident is connected to broader issues within the Australian community, as seen in the controversy surrounding Peter Dutton's comments on pro-Palestine rallies, reflecting deep divisions in Australia's response to protests with antisemitic elements. Dutton's proposal to deport non-citizens who engaged in antisemitic chants during these protests, such as 'F the Jews', 'F Israel', and waving ISIS flags, was labeled "dangerous and misleading" by Bilal Rauf of the Australian National Imams Council, who criticized it for inflaming rather than resolving tensions.

Conversely, Jeremy Leibler from the Zionist Federation of Australia supported these stringent measures, underlining the severity of the situation. This discourse on handling public expression versus maintaining community safety continues to stir debate (Karp; Butler, 2023).

Adding to the complexity of Dutton's political maneuvers, his remarks during an address at the Sydney Opera House, where he compared the social impact of pro-Palestine protests to the Port Arthur massacre -Australia's deadliest shooting- sparked further controversy. Published in The Guardian by Sarah Basford Canales on April 12, 2024, this comparison drew sharp rebukes from various sectors, including political figures and survivors.

Critics like Tasmanian Liberal MP Bridget Archer and Premier Jeremy Rockliff denounced the comparison as inappropriate and insensitive, stressing that the historical gravity of Port Arthur should not serve as a tool for contemporary political rhetoric. A massacre survivor described Dutton's remarks as 'tone deaf,' illustrating the potential harm such comparisons might inflict on those still impacted by past tragedies.

The backlash against Dutton's comments underscores the challenges leaders face in addressing sensitive issues. By drawing parallels between unrelated and highly emotive events, Dutton inadvertently highlighted the difficulties in navigating public discourse that respects the seriousness of historical events while engaging with current political and social issues. This situation showcases the delicate balance required in political communication, especially when it intersects with national traumas and ongoing societal debates.

In response to the significant rise in antisemitism in Australia, Australian lawmakers have enacted landmark legislation banning public performances of the Nazi salute and the display or sale of Nazi symbols like the swastika. Announced by Attorney-General Mark Dreyfus, these new laws also criminalize the glorification or praise of acts of terrorism. Offenders could face up to 12 months in prison. This legislative action aims to address the alarming increase in antisemitic incidents, especially in the aftermath of the October 7 terror attack by Hamas on southern Israel, which triggered a severe response from Israel.

Data from the Executive Council of Australian Jewry highlights those antisemitic incidents in Australia significantly increased during October and November 2023, with 662 incidents reported, compared to 495 in the previous

12 months. The urgency of these laws reflects the government's commitment to combating hate and ensuring community safety amidst growing concerns over antisemitic rhetoric, including incidents where chants such as 'Gas the Jews' were reported at a pro-Palestinian rally in Sydney. Prime Minister Anthony Albanese has publicly condemned these expressions of hate as 'horrific' and 'unacceptable' (E. Lyons, 2024).

At the federal level, Jewish Labor parliamentarians including Attorney-General Mark Dreyfus have been seen as disappointing by parts of the Jewish community, who also express disillusionment with Prime Minister Anthony Albanese and Foreign Minister Penny Wong's efforts to curb antisemitism. Criticisms extend to the broader Muslim community, with claims that their leaders have not adequately denounced violence or integrated into Australian society. This sentiment is coupled with concerns about the safety of the Jewish community and broader frustrations expressed by some Australians regarding the integration of Muslim residents.

Amid these tensions, Co-CEO of the Executive Council of Australian Jewry (ECAJ), Peter Wertheim, criticized the inadequacies of current hate speech and incitement to violence laws, citing several disturbing incidents where no legal actions were taken. "Since section 93Z of the Crimes Act came into effect in 2018, a neo-Nazi group in NSW has publicly stated: 'it is time to legalize the Kike Cull', anti-Israel demonstrators at the Opera House have yelled 'F the Jews', and self-styled Islamic hate preachers in Western Sydney have delivered sermons characterizing Jews as 'bloodthirsty monsters'," Wertheim highlighted.

He emphasized the disconnect between public expectations and legal standards, pointing out that "No charges have been laid and no prosecutions have been instituted in respect of those incidents," and concluded that the public is left to use its own resources for protection due to the state's failure to act (AJN, 2024).

Building on these concerns, David Ossip, President of the NSW Jewish Board of Deputies, also expressed concerns about the impact of unchecked hate speech, particularly from hate preachers who "poison the minds of their adherents by vilifying other Australians and calling for jihad." Ossip underscored the danger of such rhetoric, noting, "Such sermons are incredibly dangerous and are completely inconsistent with our Australian values," and stressed the importance of maintaining communal cohesion and harmony in the face of such threats.

In conclusion, this section underscores a critical period in Australian society where the intersection of local protests and global conflicts has notably amplified instances of antisemitism. The escalation of pro-Palestinian protests, often merging diverse groups with varying motivations, has not only intensified public discourse around Israeli-Palestinian tensions but has also influenced the safety and societal integration of Jewish communities in Australia.

These demonstrations, while aiming to protest Israeli policies, have sometimes shifted into arenas where antisemitic sentiments are expressed, impacting the Jewish community's sense of security, and belonging.

As Australia grapples with these complex issues, the path forward involves a multifaceted approach. Firstly, there is an evident need for stronger legislative measures to address hate speech and incitement more effectively. Recent actions, such as the prohibition of Nazi symbols and the Nazi salute, signify a robust governmental response to the rise in hate-driven incidents.

However, continuous evaluation and adaptation of these laws are essential to ensure they effectively curb the propagation of hate while respecting freedoms of speech and protest. Moreover, enhancing educational efforts to foster an understanding of antisemitism's impact on individuals and communities could promote empathy and counteract the spread of misinformation and biased narratives.

Ultimately, maintaining Australia's commitment to multiculturalism and social cohesion requires the active engagement of all sectors of society, including governmental bodies, community leaders, and individual citizens, in dialogue and actions that reinforce the nation's core values of diversity and inclusiveness.

By confronting these challenges head-on and addressing the root causes of antisemitism and other forms of prejudice, Australia can hope to not only mitigate the current tensions but also strengthen its social fabric for the future.

Chapter One Conclusion.

The alarming resurgence of antisemitism across the nation paints a vivid picture of the challenges and the widespread impact on the Jewish community and broader Australian society. Through detailed analysis and personal accounts, the chapter underscores the urgent need for collective action and systemic change to address this deep-seated prejudice.

It highlights the critical role of educational initiatives, legal reforms, and community engagement in combating antisemitism, urging a united front to preserve Australia's values of diversity and inclusivity. This chapter serves as a clarion call to action, advocating for a society that not only recognizes the multifaceted nature of antisemitism but also actively works towards eradicating its presence, ensuring that Australia remains a beacon of multicultural harmony and respect.

Antisemitic incidents have a profound and detrimental impact on the lives of individual Australian Jews, extending far beyond immediate physical safety concerns. The psychological toll of enduring verbal abuse, harassment, and intimidation can be severe, particularly for those who are survivors of the Holocaust or have family histories deeply affected by past atrocities. Research indicates that exposure to racism, including antisemitic rhetoric, can have lasting and severe health consequences.

This exposure has been linked to increased rates of hypertension, nightmares, post-traumatic stress disorder (PTSD), psychosis, and tragically, even suicide among affected individuals. Additionally, the use of inflammatory and hateful language can contribute to a climate where violent behavior is normalized, potentially leading to physical harm and further endangerment of Jewish communities.

The impact of antisemitic rhetoric, therefore, extends well beyond words, directly affecting the mental and physical well-being of those targeted, and highlighting the urgent need for comprehensive measures to address and prevent such incidents.

Chapter Two

From Hatred to Annihilation

The Global Reality of Antisemitism

Introduction.

Antisemitism, an ancient prejudice, has metamorphosed into a complex global phenomenon with profound implications. This chapter undertakes a comprehensive exploration of contemporary antisemitism, dissecting its multifaceted nature, examining its various manifestations in different contexts, and analyzing its reverberations across societies worldwide. The horrendous attack on Israel on October 7 has further inflated antisemitism globally, highlighting the urgent need to address this escalating issue.

Commencing with an in-depth analysis of Israel's existential conflict, the chapter illuminates the intricate web of challenges posed by pro-Iranian militias and elements of the Muslim Brotherhood. This conflict, accentuated by the pivotal role of the Iron Dome missile defense system, not only shapes Israel's security strategies but also casts a pervasive shadow over Jewish communities worldwide, sparking a troubling resurgence of antisemitic sentiments.

Transitioning from the specific to the broader ramifications, the narrative then transitions to the impact of the October 7 attacks on Western societies. This section illuminates the interconnectedness between global incidents and local repercussions, shedding light on the escalating pattern of antisemitism and its transformative effects on Jewish communities worldwide. It advocates for a holistic approach encompassing comprehensive education and robust preventive measures to counteract this escalating trend.

Delving further into the religious and ideological roots of antisemitism, the chapter proceeds to dissect its foundations within Islam. It critically examines the negative portrayal of Jews in Islamic scripture and tradition, highlighting the potential for these narratives to fuel antisemitic beliefs among Muslim communities. Emphasizing the imperative for a multifaceted strategy, including education, community engagement, and conflict resolution efforts, this section advocates for proactive measures to combat antisemitism and extremist rhetoric within the Muslim sphere.

Finally, the chapter scrutinizes the proliferation of radical preachers within Australia's Muslim communities, which poses a formidable threat not only to the safety and security of Jewish communities but to broader Australian society as well. It raises concerns about the emergence of a hostile environment reminiscent of a '**Mini-Middle East**,' where antisemitism escalates from hatred to the potential annihilation of Jews. This underscores the urgent need for authorities to acknowledge and promptly address this burgeoning threat.

In conclusion, this chapter offers a comprehensive examination of the global reach of antisemitism, tracing its evolution from rhetoric to reality. It underscores the imperative for proactive and multifaceted strategies to combat this insidious phenomenon, emphasizing the crucial role of education, dialogue, policy, and conflict resolution in fostering a more inclusive and peaceful world.

2.1 Beneath the Iron Dome: Overview of Israel's Existential Conflict.

Israel faces a severe existential conflict, grappling with formidable threats from pro-Iranian militias and elements of the Muslim Brotherhood intent on eradicating its statehood. This dire situation has escalated to a critical juncture, emphasizing the indispensable role of the Iron Dome missile defense system, which has been crucial in mitigating losses since hostilities resumed on October 7. Rooted in deep existential fears, this conflict shapes Israel's security and diplomatic strategies, profoundly influencing its approach to regional threats.

Further exacerbating these challenges, pro-Iranian militias and factions strategically located in Iraq, Syria, Lebanon, and Yemen significantly threaten Israel's existence. These groups, aligned with Iran's strategic interests, have intensified their activities, thereby escalating security concerns across the region. The operations and existential challenges posed by these militias, such as Kataib Hezbollah and Kataib Sayyid al-Shuhada in Iraq and Syria, are pivotal in understanding the ongoing tensions.

These groups have not only formed a 'resistance operations room' with Hamas but their radical stance and strong ties to Iran categorize them as formidable adversaries capable of attacking U.S. interests and directly threatening Israel through strategic alliances (Furlan, 2022; Sallon 2023).

Additionally, the Badr Organization and Asaib Ahl al-Haq in Iraq, historically backed by Iran, have opposed Israeli actions in Gaza. Their significant political influence within the Iraqi government and alignment with Iran's goals make them key players in the region. In Lebanon, Hezbollah, part of the Iran-led 'Axis of Evil,' directly threatens Israel's security by supporting Palestinian rights (Harel, 2024).

Hezbollah's leader, Hassan Nasrallah, has vocally affirmed his organization's staunch opposition to recognizing Israel, describing it as a usurping, racist, aggressor, and terrorist state, and claims Hezbollah can potentially eliminate Israel from existence. For further reading on the Hezbollah threat to northern Israel, refer to the analysis by the Center for Strategic and International Studies (CSIS) titled 'The Coming Conflict with Hezbollah' by Seth G. Jones et al.

Similarly, the Houthis in Yemen, part of this axis and supported by Iran, express solidarity with Hamas, adding complexity to the regional conflicts that not only threatens Israel's security but also impact Jewish communities globally. These groups, ideologically and materially supported by Iran, form a network that not only allows Iran to exert influence but also poses a multifaceted threat to Israel's existence, underscoring the critical security challenges Israel faces in a volatile geopolitical landscape (Schaer, 2023).

Christine Kensche, a Middle East correspondent for the German newspaper Die Welt, has documented Iran's extensive support for a network of militant groups. This network, bolstered by weapons, funding, and training from Tehran, is part of Iran's strategy to destabilize U.S. interests and target Israel. Western intelligence services and financial investigations reveal that Iran's backing extends beyond the usual Shiite and Sunni factions to include a variety of groups with no direct connections to Israel or fundamentalist Islam. This includes from disbanded Jihadist organizations to the Polisario Front in North Africa (Abascal, 2023).

Furthermore, Iran utilizes the Al Quds Brigades, the international operations wing of the Revolutionary Guards, to collaborate with groups like Hamas in Gaza, amplifying the threats against Israel. Under Iran's influence, these groups actively promote narratives centered on the annihilation of the Jewish state, thereby heightening the existential threat to Israel amidst the ongoing Gaza conflict. In response to these coordinated threats, Israel has targeted key figures within the Islamic Revolutionary Guard Corps (IRGC) who are instrumental outside Iran.

This includes proportionate military responses and surgical operations that have neutralized high-profile individuals such as Qassim Soleimani, Mohammad Reza Zahedi, and Reza Mousavi, among several other brigadiers. These figures were specifically targeted due to their roles in supplying logistics to pro-Iranian militias that threaten the Israeli state and its communities, underlining the strategic defense measures Israel deems necessary to safeguard its sovereignty and security (Gavlak, 2024).

This aggressive posture is further substantiated by a direct statement from the leader of Hamas, who confirmed Iran's substantial support to the Al-Qassam Brigades and other resistance factions. Yahya Sinwar (2023) highlighted the significant financial, logistical, and technical assistance that has markedly enhanced their capabilities. This support, he emphasized, fuels their opposition to normalization efforts with Israel, which he claims starkly opposes the core values of their nation and people. Corroborating this, Joby Warrick (2023) has noted that Iran not only trains these groups but is also the primary backer of their activities, extending from the Red Sea to the Atlantic Ocean, emphasizing its role in regional terror activities.

Among these various resistance factions in Gaza, Hamas is the most prominent. It originated from the Muslim Brotherhood during the First Intifada and seized control of Gaza in 2007 after clashing with the Fatah faction. The military capabilities of Hamas are significantly enhanced by its Izz ad-Din al-Qassam Brigades. Alongside Hamas, groups like the Palestinian Islamic Jihad's Al-Quds Brigades and the Popular Resistance Committees' Al-Nasser Salah Ad-Din Brigades also play substantial roles, reflecting considerable Iranian influence in the region.

These groups receive logistical and military support from Iran and are part of larger regional networks resisting the Jewish state, contributing to the ongoing security threats faced by Israel. This intricate nexus of alliances and support illustrates the complex and enduring nature of the conflict in the region (O'Connor, 2023).

Beyond disrupting normalization efforts and threatening nearby communities and Kibbutzim, these Gaza-based terrorist factions launched attacks on October 7 with the additional intent of capturing civilian hostages and military personnel. This strategy aimed to bolster their bargaining position for a future exchange deal, mirroring the 2011 Gilad Shalit swap. Their overarching goal was to replicate Hamas's structure, training, and weapons manufacturing capabilities into the West Bank, thereby escalating threats to Israel's existence and further destabilizing the state by reintegrating influential prisoners who previously held sway in the West Bank, more so than the Palestinian Authority (PA).

An Israeli report disclosed some key figures whom the Palestinian Hamas movement seeks to release from Israeli prisons, as part of a proposed truce that would include releasing hostages currently held in Gaza. According to The Times of Israel, which cited a report from Hebrew Channel 12, Hamas's list is expected to include Palestinian prisoners serving life sentences for their roles in major attacks during the second Palestinian intifada between 2000 and 2005. Notable names on this list include the Barghouti brothers, Abbas Al-Sayyed, Ibrahim Hamed, Ahmed Saadat, and Muhammad Arman, underscoring the significant implications of such a deal on regional security dynamics (Staff, 2024).

These regional security dynamics stemming from the actions and ideologies of groups like Hamas have far-reaching implications that extend beyond Israel to impact several Arab states, including Morocco, Saudi Arabia, Jordan, and the United Arab Emirates. These groups, often inspired by the teachings of Sayed Qutb and the broader ideology of the Muslim Brotherhood, not only advocate for the elimination of the Israeli state but also call for the overthrow of Arab governments that they deem un-Islamic.

Their ultimate aim is the establishment of a Caliphate governed by a single ruler, a Caliph. This ideology poses a significant threat to the stability of these nations, prompting leaders from these countries to align closely with figures like Israeli Prime Minister Netanyahu, who is seen as a bulwark against such uprisings. Their support is driven by a fear of insurrection similar to the Arab Spring, which threatened many reigning governments in the region (Times of Israel, 2024).

This strategic alignment underscores a complex interplay of regional politics where Arab leaders, despite their public rhetoric, often prioritize internal security and regime stability over outward ideological alignments. The threat of extremist ideologies leading to popular uprisings is a palpable concern that influences their foreign policy and diplomatic relations, including with Israel. The need for stability and control motivates these leaders to support measures that can prevent the spread of revolutionary Islamist ideologies that threaten their rule and the current political order.

In Saudi Arabia, public demonstrations are strictly prohibited, and those attempting to organize them are swiftly arrested for betraying the regime. Speaking out against normalization with Israel is also forbidden, with over 400 people reportedly jailed for doing so. This exemplifies the lengths to which some Arab governments go to maintain stability and suppress dissent, even as they navigate complex regional dynamics and diplomatic relationships (Perry, 2024).

In Sum, the October 7th attacks showcased the complexity of identifying assailants from multiple factions involved in various violent acts such as killings, rapes, hostage-takings, and arsons. This ambiguity allows these groups to deny any involvement, especially in heinous acts like rape. Post-attack, many assailants blend back into civilian life, working in bakeries, schools, hospitals, news agencies, media outlets, charities, and government offices, thereby complicating the distinction between combatants and non-combatants. This dual role was highlighted in footage from the attacks, depicting a cross-section of Gaza's society engaging in hostilities, dressed in everyday clothing.

Moreover, the harrowing accounts of former hostages Nili Margalit and Mia Schem further expose the deep-seated hostilities within Gaza. Margalit reported being abducted from her home in Nir Oz by Palestinian Arab civilians, then sold to Hamas members. This incident underscores the pervasive involvement of the local population in the hostilities.

Schem, captured while attending the Nova music festival, described her experience on Israeli television as encountering 'pure hatred.' She emphasized that in Gaza, indoctrination against Jews starts in early childhood, stating, "There are no innocent citizens there. They are families controlled by Hamas. There are children who from the moment they are born are taught that Israel is Palestine and just to hate Jews." These testimonies illustrate the profound impact of the conflict on individual lives and further blur the lines between civilians and combatants within the region (Jewish Chronicle, 2024).

In a statement, the IDF claimed freed hostages Almog Meir Jan, Andrey Kozlov, and Shlomi Ziv were held by journalist Abdallah Aljamal and his family members at their home in the central Gaza Nuseirat camp. Aljamal, an alleged Al-Jazeera journalist, lived on the first floor of a multi-story building, according to Euro-Med. The IDF reported the hostages were found on the third floor. According to Joshua Marks (2024),

Abdallah's family home held hostages alongside family members.

This is further proof that the Hamas terrorist organization uses the civilian population as a human shield. The harrowing testimonies of these freed hostages, coupled with the IDF's findings, irrefutably demonstrate the extent to which Hamas exploits the civilian populace for their nefarious purposes, thus cementing the organization's culpability in perpetuating terror and suffering in the region.

Given these findings and the pervasive threats posed by Hamas, the Israeli Defense Forces (IDF) have adopted a strategy of targeting entities identified as 'terrorist infrastructure,' such as the Al-Shifa hospital, schools, and facilities run by the United Nations Relief and Works Agency (UNRWA). These military actions, aimed at neutralizing Hamas and associated threats, have unfortunately resulted in substantial civilian casualties, including women and children. The strikes underscore the profound challenges faced by the IDF in a densely populated combat zone, reflecting the harsh realities of modern urban warfare where combat zones and tunnels are intertwined with civilian areas.

As the conflict continues, the IDF confronts not just Hamas, but a broader coalition of Palestinian factions committed to eradicating Israel. These factions collaborate through joint operations and issue collective statements against Israel, indicating a unified resistance. IDF Colonel Moshe Tetro emphasized during a press conference that dismantling the Hamas regime is a priority given its substantial military capabilities within Gaza. He clearly stated, "Our objective is to demolish the terror regime of Hamas," highlighting Hamas as the primary threat.

However, he also noted that any armed opposition, including groups like Islamic Jihad, which he pointed out as lacking a political presence in Gaza and focusing solely on military actions, would also be targeted. This policy illustrates the IDF's comprehensive approach to countering all armed resistance within the region, reinforcing Israel's strategic defense initiatives during an ongoing, complex conflict that presents continuous threats to its national security and the safety of its citizens.

In Conclusion, this existential conflict faced by Israel, epitomized by the October 7 attacks, not only emphasizes the security dilemmas within its borders but also casts a long shadow on Jewish communities worldwide, particularly in the West including Australia. The violence and rhetoric from these attacks have stirred deep-seated antisemitic sentiments globally, manifesting in various forms such as harassment, boycotts, and violent protests. Chants like 'Gaz the Jews,' 'Death to Israel,' and 'Zionists don't deserve to live' are not just slogans; they reflect a disturbing escalation of hatred that transcends geographical boundaries, affecting Jews far from the immediate zones of conflict.

This resurgence of antisemitism in the West is further complicated by the portrayal of these conflicts in media and public discourse, which often simplifies the nuanced geopolitical realities into binary narratives. Such simplifications can inadvertently validate antisemitic sentiments, presenting them as legitimate political criticisms.

This phenomenon highlights the broader implications of Israel's existential threats, underscoring not only the physical security concerns for the state itself but also the safety and well-being of Jewish populations globally. The international community's response to these developments remains pivotal in shaping the future trajectory of both regional stability and the global fight against rising antisemitic rhetoric and violence.

2.2 From Conflict to Community: The Ripple Effects of October 7 in the Western World.

The October 7 attack on Israel significantly impacted Western societies, revealing the deep interconnectedness between global incidents and local consequences. This event not only led to a resurgence of antisemitic incidents, as highlighted by Heidi Beirich of the Global Project Against Hate and Extremism, but also provoked a broad international response, including a stern condemnation from U.S. President Joe Biden (Lapin, 2024). The attack underscored the volatile nature of geopolitical tensions and their capacity to catalyze widespread societal and political shifts across Western nations.

In Europe, the reaction was marked by a sharp increase in antisemitic activities and enhanced security measures around Jewish communities. For instance, in Sarcelles, France, known as 'Little Jerusalem,' the local Jewish population experienced significant disruptions, with businesses like

Jeremy's restaurant suffering due to safety concerns (Caulcutt; Economist, 2024).

The response extended to Germany, where Chancellor Olaf Scholz's zero-tolerance policy towards antisemitism followed incidents like the Star of David being daubed on buildings in Berlin, an act laden with historical and painful connotations (Marsh, 2023). These events across various European nations, including Austria and Belgium, where antisemitic acts surged, illustrate the broader pattern of increased threats and security challenges faced by Jewish communities in the wake of the October 7 attacks.

In a related development, protests erupted in Malmo, Sweden, where demonstrators, including prominent figures like Gretta Thunberg, called for the destruction of Israel and the deportation of Jews back to Poland. The atmosphere grew tense as protesters chanted, 'Sinwar, we will not let you die,' referring to the military leader of Hamas.

The situation escalated when Ynet reporter Zeev Avrahami, covering the events for the news outlet, was attacked by participants demanding he prove he is not Jewish or Israeli. Avrahami's experience reflects a broader trend of violence and intimidation faced by Jews and journalists in the region (Avrahami, 2024).

Meanwhile, in Geneva, Switzerland, Israeli student Noam Sayag reported feeling unsafe due to the alarming prevalence of antisemitic sentiments. Sayag, who is studying at the Geneva School of Diplomacy, expressed grave concerns over the hostile environment. He noted that pro-Palestinian protesters distributed flags emblazoned with swastikas and sang songs calling for the 'rape of Jewish women,' creating a climate of fear and intimidation. Another Jewish student, Shir, voiced worries about the potential impact of boycotts on her medical degree, illustrating the broader ramifications of antisemitic actions on academic pursuits and professional futures (Avrahami, 2024).

In similar vein, In June 2024, the Belgian arts center Monty Hall in Antwerp canceled a Jewish school's event over the Gaza war, citing Israel's alleged 'genocide.' The head of this municipally funded center vowed not to cooperate with the Israeli government 'or any organization associated with it,' further entrenching antisemitic sentiments. Rabbi Menachem Margolin, director of the European Jewish Association, condemned the center's actions and called on the city government to terminate its subsidies, denouncing the director's blatant "racism and antisemitism." (Reyes, 2024).

The cancellation in Antwerp is among numerous cases where European artistic and academic institutions have canceled or attempted to cancel events associated with Israel following Hamas's October 7 attack on southern Israel. These incidents starkly highlight the escalating challenges faced by Jewish individuals in Europe, underscoring the urgent need for heightened awareness and decisive action to combat the rising tide of antisemitism. The persistent targeting of Jewish communities as scapegoats for geopolitical conflicts reflects a deep-seated prejudice that continues to jeopardize their safety and well-being.

In Canada, Prime Minister Justin Trudeau expressed grave concerns about the rise in antisemitic incidents, emphasizing the severity of the burgeoning antisemitic trends across the nation. His administration's response has been proactive, focusing on addressing direct threats and acts of aggression against the Jewish community. A notable incident that triggered this strong response was the attempted arson at Congregation Beth Tikvah synagogue in Montreal (MacDonald, 2023). This alarming event not only emphasized the immediate dangers faced by Jewish Canadians but also served as a catalyst for government and local authorities to intensify their efforts in combating hate crimes.

Another distressing case involved Eitan Cohen, a 13-year-old Israeli student who faced relentless bullying and harassment from his Muslim classmates in Toronto. The situation escalated to a horrifying extent, with students telling him, "They want to do to him what Hamas did to Israel," and even going so far as to say, "Hitler's work needs to be finished," followed by physical violence, including beating and stoning. Despite his parents' repeated complaints, the school administration failed to take adequate measures, leading to accusations of complicity in the bullying.

In response, hundreds of members of the Jewish community in Toronto came together to escort Eitan to school, providing a much-needed sense of safety and security. This act of solidarity and support was a powerful reminder of the importance of community and collective action in the face of antisemitism, and it underscores the urgent need for schools to implement more robust measures to protect Jewish students and address antisemitic behavior promptly and effectively (Holt, 2024).

In the United States, the Anti-Defamation League (ADL) reported a significant surge in antisemitic incidents in 2023, with a record 140% increase from the previous year. This disturbing rise, which averaged 24 anti-Jewish incidents per day, totaling 8,873 cases of assault, harassment, and vandalism, was largely attributed to the ongoing conflict in Gaza. The ADL's comprehensive audit revealed a particularly stark increase in antisemitic activities on college campuses, where incidents escalated by 321%, and in non-Jewish K-12 schools, with 1,162 incidents reflecting a 135% increase. Jewish institutions saw a 237% rise in targeted attacks, with bomb threats predominating during the fall, mainly targeting synagogues which accounted for 73% of all institutional incidents (ADL, 2024).

Additionally, the alarming rise in antisemitic incidents and organized white supremacist activities documented by the Anti-Defamation League illustrates a troubling national trend. With 1,161 antisemitic propaganda distributions noted last year, incidents concentrated heavily in states with large Jewish populations such as California, New York, New Jersey, Florida, and Massachusetts.

This surge underscores a significant increase in rhetoric that equates Jewish identities or Zionist affiliations with extremist positions. In response to these dire statistics, the ADL, led by Jonathan Greenblatt and Oren Segal, has urged robust action at both state and national levels to counteract this rise in antisemitism and foster community resilience and proactive law enforcement engagement.

This national context provides a backdrop for understanding specific instances of antisemitism, such as the disturbing incident at Origins High School in Brooklyn reported by Susan Edelman. Approximately three weeks after the Hamas attack on Israel, a group of 40 to 50 teenagers marched through the school, chanting "Death to Israel!" and "Kill the Jews!" This act of intimidation at the school level reflects the broader trend of increasing antisemitism and is emblematic of the challenges that communities face, emphasizing the need for continued vigilance and comprehensive strategies to address these threats and harassments.

The severity of the harassment includes students mimicking Hitler, drawing swastikas, making death threats towards Jewish staff members, such as teacher Danielle Kaminsky, and one teen even expressing a disturbing intent "to have sex with a dead Jewish woman". These actions have created a climate of fear and hostility, exacerbated by the administration's insufficient response to discipline the offenders effectively.

Despite these ongoing incidents, the interim acting principal, Dara Kammerman, has primarily relied on contacting parents and attempting 'restorative justice,' without significant repercussions for the perpetrators. This approach has raised concerns among staff and advocates about the perpetuation of an antisemitic environment within the school, prompting calls for more decisive actions to address and prevent further harassment.

As we consider the various sources and manifestations of antisemitism within Western societies, it's important to also examine the role of pro-Palestinian protests, which have contributed to the intensification of antisemitic rhetoric. These protests, while often rooted in legitimate political expression related to the Israeli-Palestinian conflict, can unfortunately spill over into overt antisemitism. Incidents during such demonstrations have included the use of inflammatory rhetoric such as 'Death to Israel' and 'Gaz the Jews,' which not only stigmatizes the Jewish community but also conflates Jewish identities globally with the actions of the Israeli government.

This conflation can exacerbate tensions and foster an environment where antisemitism flourishes under the guise of political protest. As such, these demonstrations, particularly in the wake of the October 7 attacks, have highlighted the thin line between political activism and harmful antisemitic discourse, underscoring the complexity of responding to and addressing these incidents within a framework that respects free expression while vigorously countering hate.

On November 11, 2023, a significant pro-Palestinian protest in London led to the detention of over 100 demonstrators by the Metropolitan Police for behaviors including launching fireworks and wearing Hamas face coverings. This protest, occurring on Armistice Day, elicited strong reactions from both the public and officials, with Prime Minister Rishi Sunak denouncing the disruptive actions of both far-right and pro-Palestinian protesters. He emphasized that such behaviors deeply disrespected the commemoration of the armed forces.

During the march, demonstrators were reported to chant "Death to Israel!" and "Kill the Jews!", a rhetoric that not only alarmed due to its explicit violence but also echoed deeply rooted antisemitic sentiments. Furthermore, the chant "from the river to the sea, Palestine will be free" was also heard, a phrase many Jewish groups consider a call for the eradication of Israel and inherently antisemitic (Reuters, 2023).

The implications of these protests on societal antisemitism were further highlighted in a subsequent demonstration on March 31, 2024, as reported by Tom Cheshire. The intense standoff between pro-Palestinian marchers and a smaller group of pro-Israeli counter-protesters in London was fraught with ideological conflict. The pro-Palestinian group's use of the contentious slogan "From the River to the Sea" not only amplified the protest's confrontational nature but also underscored its potential to foster antisemitic attitudes.

Such incidents, including a throat-slashing gesture made by a pro-Palestinian protester towards a counter-protester draped in an Israeli flag, underscore the palpable threats posed by these confrontations. This climate of heightened animosity and ideological clashes not only challenges law enforcement's capacity to maintain public order but also reflects the broader societal implications where political expressions can sometimes exacerbate antisemitic prejudices, highlighting a critical area of concern for community relations and national security.

Ironically, despite the prevalence of antisemitic slogans and graffiti in the UK, some Jihadi buffoons were not content with mere words; they felt compelled to arm themselves with AK-47s and execute their Jewish neighbors. Two men, Walid Saadaoui and Amar Hussein, appeared in a British court, charged with planning to use automatic weapons to attack and kill members of the Jewish community and others in northwest England.

This disturbing development, part of a trend of rising antisemitic crime levels, has been condemned by the Community Security Trust (CST), a Jewish security advisory body. The CST emphasized the necessity of extensive security measures for the Jewish community and underscored the importance of their partnership with police and government.

This incident serves as a poignant illustration of the alarming reality of global antisemitism, which has escalated from mere hatred to calls for annihilation. It underscores the urgent need for measures such as the 'Safety of Rwanda Bill' in Britain, which permits the deportation of certain immigrants to Rwanda. The irony lies in the fact that while such legislation aims to enhance safety and security, The Muslim Council of Britain has criticized the government's controversial deportation proposals. This contradiction highlights the complexities and challenges of addressing issues of security and immigration in a context where antisemitic sentiments and threats persist.

Furthermore, the discourse surrounding the Israel-Hamas war has significantly heightened the debate on college campuses across the United States, intertwining issues of free speech and antisemitism. As Anna Betts (2024) reports, many Jewish students and alumni are alarmed, perceiving those pro-Palestinian protests occasionally cross into antisemitic rhetoric and violence. This perception has prompted a notable increase in investigations by the Department of Education's Office for Civil Rights, looking into allegations of antisemitism in both college and K-12 settings, significantly more than in previous years.

Additionally, this situation has led the Republican-led House Committee on Education and the Workforce to begin investigations and hold hearings. These governmental actions have resulted in substantial administrative changes at renowned institutions such as Harvard and the University of Pennsylvania.

The ensuing debates and protests underscore deep divisions within academic communities, reflecting broader global tensions related to the Israel-Hamas conflict. This divisive atmosphere is manifested through various campus activities, including the resignations of university presidents and student protests, which sometimes lead to campus closures, highlighting the complex dynamics between academic freedom, political activism, and community relations in higher education.

At Columbia University, rising tensions due to pro-Palestinian protests have significantly heightened safety concerns for Jewish students. In response to these concerns, Columbia's President, Nemat Shafik, announced the transition to virtual classes to address the immediate crisis, underlining the severe impact of these demonstrations. This decision was precipitated by notable incidents of antisemitic threats and harassment, including reports of students being aggressively told to "go back to Poland" and accusations of harming children, which have intensified fears among Jewish students for their personal safety (Romero, 2024).

The protests at Columbia, characterized by accusations and inflammatory rhetoric, have tested the boundaries of free speech and safety, leading the university to implement heightened security measures. The situation escalated when a protest leader, Khymani James, was banned from campus for stating, "Zionists don't deserve to live," underscoring the intensity of the anti-Zionist sentiment among demonstrators. This incident highlights the challenges institutions face in balancing free speech with the need to maintain a safe and inclusive environment for all community members, particularly those of Jewish descent who may feel targeted or threatened by such rhetoric (Staff, 2024).

These security measures include the recruitment of additional personnel and stricter ID checks, especially during sensitive periods such as Passover. The responses from the university and local authorities emphasize the significant impact such demonstrations can have. While rooted in political expression, they can sometimes manifest as overt antisemitism, profoundly affecting the campus climate and Jewish students' sense of security.

The incident at Columbia underscores the need for ongoing efforts to address antisemitism and ensure that universities remain spaces where diverse perspectives can be expressed without fear of harassment or discrimination. This context of rising antisemitic rhetoric and its impact on campus environments further underscores the urgency of implementing effective security measures and promoting inclusivity and tolerance within educational institutions.

Similarly, in a May 18, 2024, D.C. march on the National Mall commemorating the Nakba, pro-Palestinian protesters in the United States vehemently called for the annihilation of Israel, Zionism, and Jewish lobbies within the state. Speakers at the event expressed a clear shift in rhetoric from mere hatred to outright calls for annihilation. They chanted slogans such as "Palestine is ours alone! We don't want two states, we're taking back '48!" and called for Jihad and suicidal inclinations towards martyrdom, stating "We say: Victory or martyrdom, and with every martyr that joins the ranks in the Heavens, a new fighter rises." This alarming escalation in antisemitic rhetoric underscores the urgent need to condemn such hateful speech.

Organizers and speakers at the march, including those from Maryland2Palestine and the Palestinian Youth Movement, explicitly stated that their goal is not a ceasefire but the total liberation of Palestine and the end of the "76-year Zionist occupation." They rejected the idea of peace talks and called for resistance against what they described as the imperialism, white supremacy, and disease of Zionism. This event highlights the dangerous path of antisemitism that some elements within the pro-Palestinian movement have taken, demonstrating a concerning disregard for the rights and security of the Jewish people (Khalil, 2024).

Comparably, on June 8, 2024, there was a demonstration in front of the White House attended by thousands of pro-Palestinian protesters, where chants calling for 'Death to Israel' and advocating Jihad against the country were heard. Many protesters marched with their faces covered in keffiyehs, chanting slogans in support of Hamas military wing, such as 'Kill another soldier now,' and cheering for Hezbollah to 'Kill another Zionist now,' along with calls for a violent uprising.

Some protesters took over a statue in front of the White House, with one masked protester burning a U.S. flag, while hundreds of others vandalized the statue, sprayed anti-Israel and anti-U.S. graffiti, and threw paint and objects at it while a police officer attempted to protect it (TOI, 2024).

The clips and images from the demonstration prompted strong reactions against the protesters for vandalizing statues and America's liberal values and national symbols. People called on the police to prosecute the protesters, imprison them, and take severe action against their families. The strong reactions against the protesters underscore the deep-seated concerns regarding the protection of America's liberal values and national symbols.

The calls for prosecution, imprisonment, and severe action against the protesters reflect a broader societal concern over the perceived threats posed by acts of vandalism and disrespect towards these symbols. This incident highlights the complex intersection of freedom of expression, political activism, and the protection of national identity, prompting a critical examination of how such tensions can be navigated within a democratic society.

Worse yet, it is plausible that Iranian brigadiers and spiritual leaders are closely observing these protests, potentially seeking to embrace and enlist antisemitic elements, much as they have done with previous Jihadi factions. They have a track record of organizing, training, and radicalizing such groups, channeling their anger and hatred into tangible acts of terror. This situation should serve as both an eye-opener and a warning to US intelligence and security agencies. They should intensify their monitoring of radical preachers and instigators, considering a combination of soft and hard measures to ensure national safety and security, with particular attention to American Jewish communities and lobbies.

In Conclusion, this increasing pattern of antisemitism, as documented by significant organizations like the ADL, provides a crucial context for understanding the profound personal and communal impacts of these incidents. The aftermath of these attacks has been deeply transformative for Jews worldwide, altering perceptions of identity, safety, and affiliations with Israel. Divisions within the community have intensified, affecting personal relationships and altering political stances, with some Jews becoming more Zionist while others turned against Zionism.

This shift has also influenced Jewish practices and expressions of identity, such as the wearing of Star of David necklaces or the removal of mezuzahs from doorposts, reflecting a community grappling with a profound crisis and questioning the once perceived sanctuary of Israel as a 'safe haven' (Maltz, 2024).

Such events not only highlight the urgent need for comprehensive education on antisemitism and the implementation of effective preventive measures but also underscore the necessity for robust enforcement and support mechanisms to protect affected communities.

Moreover, the role of pro-Palestinian protests in exacerbating antisemitic sentiments illustrates the complex interplay between legitimate political expression and the propagation of hate. These demonstrations often blur the lines between criticizing state policies and promoting antisemitic ideologies, thereby complicating efforts to address these challenges within a framework that respects free expression while actively countering expressions of hate.

2.3 Antisemitism, Boycotts, and Jihad: The Impact of Rhetoric in the Muslim Sphere.

In Islamic tradition, antisemitism is deeply rooted in scripture and tradition, distinguishing itself from other sources of hostility towards Jews, which may stem from historical grievances, ideological differences, or emotional factors. The Quran, regarded by Muslims as the direct word of Allah, often portrays Jews in a negative light. It depicts them as agitators against Muslims, exhibiting intense hostility and engaging in warfare.

Various Quranic verses attribute negative traits to Jews, such as disobedience to God, claims of wealth superiority, rejection of prophets, and engaging in lying, treachery, and covenant-breaking. Furthermore, Jews are accused of killing prophets, unjustly consuming wealth, spreading corruption, and displaying envy, immorality, stinginess, and humiliation. These portrayals contribute to a negative perception of Jews within Islamic teachings and potentially fuel antisemitic beliefs among its followers.

Contrastingly, the Quran explicitly designates the Land of Israel as the ancestral homeland of the Jewish people, a territory bestowed upon them by God Himself as an inheritance and a directive to reside there. Several verses also depict the Children of Israel as God's chosen people, divinely blessed with abundant favors such as knowledge, beauty, wealth, and intellect [Quran 2-47].

These blessings, however, are sometimes perceived as triggers for jealousy and animosity from other nations. Unfortunately, most Muslims tend to overlook these positive textual depictions of Jews, focusing instead on the negative antisemitic portrayals. This selective interpretation has led to a division within Muslim communities, with some adopting anti-Israel stances while others express support for Zionism (Margolis, 2001).

The antisemitic depictions within Islamic tradition were further exacerbated by the October 7 attack launched against Israel by a coalition of Jihadi factions. This event invoked a narrative from Islamic prophetic tradition regarding the defeat of Jews, culminating in the imagery of the last Jew being identified and killed by the awaited Imam Mahdi's Arab army, as detailed in an authentic Hadith.

The heinous nature of this attack reignited chants and slogans of "Khaybar Khaybar Ya Yahud!" across the Arab world, evoking the historic Battle of Khaybar. This battle, which occurred during the lifetime of Prophet Mohammed in 628 CE, resulted in the massacre of several Jewish tribes, the seizure of their wealth, and the enslavement of their women.

During the First Intifada, Hamas leaflets encouraged Palestinians to reinterpret the memory of Khaybar into a new conflict with Israel. The slogan "Khaybar Khaybar O Jews" has frequently appeared in Hamas demonstrations and wall graffiti. This reference to Khaybar has also been used in other conflicts involving Israel. During the Lebanon War of 2006, the Lebanese Shia militia Hezbollah dubbed missiles it fired on Israeli cities after Khaybar.

More recently, on April 13, 2024, the Islamic Revolutionary Guards Corps (IRGC) of Iran, in collaboration with other regional groups, launched retaliatory attacks against Israel and the Israeli-occupied Golan Heights, with hundreds of missiles dubbed "Khaybar Shekan," meant to invoke the annihilation of the Jewish state.

The name Khaybar has also been appropriated for a television series that portrays the hostile relations between Jews and Arabs during the historic Battle. This series has faced criticism for its negative portrayal of Jews, particularly from organizations such as the Middle East Media Research Institute (MEMRI) and the Anti-Defamation League (ADL).

Moreover, The Ijtihad and Fatwa Committee of the International Union of Muslim Scholars issued a significant verdict on October 31, 2023, condemning the aggressive actions of Zionists against Gaza. This verdict underscores the legal and moral imperative for ruling regimes and official armies to intervene to prevent genocide and widespread destruction. Declaring Jihad against Israel and support for Palestine as a legal duty, the verdict asserts that remaining silent in the face of aggression is forbidden by Sharia. It emphasizes that abandoning Gaza, Al-Aqsa, Jerusalem, and Palestine to destruction constitutes a betrayal of God, His Messenger, and the believers.

The committee calls for military intervention and the supply of equipment, highlighting the duty of the Palestinian Authority, resistance factions, and neighboring countries like Egypt, Jordan, Syria, and Lebanon to act against the Jewish state. It also urges scholars, elites, and various institutions to pressure ruling regimes and armies to fulfill their responsibilities in response to recent Zionist aggression supported by Western powers.

At the Doha 2024 conference, Sheikh Ali Muhyiddin Al-Qaradaghi, President of the International Union of Muslim Scholars, highlighted the Union's significant role in defending Palestinian rights and condemning Israeli crimes against Gaza. He mentioned the Union's efforts in mobilizing street protests and organizing a general strike across Arab and Islamic countries.

Al-Qaradaghi also praised South Africa's initiative to file a lawsuit against Israel at the International Court of Justice, criticizing the lack of support from many Arab and Islamic nations. The Union has consistently issued fatwas and statements urging preachers to remind people of the Palestinian cause and the obligation to support them against Israel, emphasizing that abandonment of Palestinians is prohibited by Islamic law.

The inflammatory rhetoric of war emanating from certain Muslim clergy and leaders of the Brotherhood, exemplified by Khalid Mashal's speech, underscores a dangerous and regressive mindset within Islamist factions. Mashal's call to arms, inciting 'fighting and combat,' and urging for 'jihad' to liberate Al-Aqsa, reveals a destructive and extremist ideology. This approach, characterized by a suicidal inclination, is exacerbated by an alarming degree of arrogance and empty rhetoric. Mashal's emphasis on seeking 'blood and lives,' rather than material resources or prayers, highlights a disturbing trend of using fabricated religious symbols to justify violence.

The Brotherhood's call for war in the name of heaven seeks to exert control over the masses through religious and racial manipulation. It is imperative to recognize the hypocrisy of those who incite conflict from the safety of their luxurious villas in Qatar, while leaving vulnerable populations exposed to the brutality of well-equipped military forces. This behavior not only endangers lives but also perpetuates a cycle of violence and instability, driven by leaders who are removed from the dire consequences of their inflammatory declarations.

Even more concerning is the shift in stance among prominent Salafi scholars, who, with millions of followers in the Islamic world, have transitioned from advocating Jihad against the Shia regimes of Syria and Iraq to expressing sympathy for the pro-Iranian militias in their attacks against Israel.

Sheikh Othman Al-Khamis initially criticized these militias, questioning the nature of their Jihad and accusing them of having a corrupt creed, praising Al-Khomeini, and pursuing their own agendas. However, he later revised his position, stating that while the Jihadi factions in Gaza may have creedal deviations, the conflict ultimately boils down to a struggle between Muslims and infidels, and it is obligatory to stand in arms with these Muslim factions.

Similarly, in a widely circulated video, Mustafa Al-Adawi, an Egyptian Salafi cleric, was observed praying for Allah to grant victory and steadfastness to Hamas. He also expressed a desire to destroy Americans and Jews, whom he perceives as spreading corruption on earth. Al-Adawi emphasized that any Muslim capable of supporting Gaza should do so through prayer, financial assistance, or by taking up arms.

This inflammatory rhetoric has the potential to incite violence and undermine the safety and security of Jewish individuals abroad. The potential consequences of Al-Adawi's statements are exemplified by recent incidents, such as the shooting that occurred on October 8, 2023, in the Sawari district of Alexandria, Egypt. In this attack, two Israeli tourists and their Egyptian guide were killed, while one Egyptian was injured. Notably, this incident marked the first such attack targeting Israelis in Egypt in decades (Reuters, 2023).

Furthermore, on May 8, 2024, a Canadian Israeli man was shot dead in Alexandria, Egypt, in a suspected criminal case. However, a known militant group claimed responsibility for the attack, citing the ongoing conflict in Gaza as the motivation. These statements and actions by Mustafa Al-Adawi have the potential to contribute to a climate of hostility and violence against Jewish individuals, particularly in regions where extremist ideologies are prevalent. It is crucial for relevant authorities and organizations to closely monitor such rhetoric and its potential consequences on global security and safety (Hassan, 2024).

Ahmed El-Tayeb, the Grand Mufti and preeminent authority of mainstream Islam, has further emphasized the paramount importance of the Palestinian cause within the Muslim world. He has expressed that history will not be forgiving to those who fail to defend oppressed Palestinians or who support the perpetuation of Zionist terrorism. El-Tayeb asserts that it is the collective duty of the Arab and Islamic nations to unite to halt Zionist expansion. He has unequivocally stated, "The belief I firmly hold is that every occupation, including Israel, will eventually disappear."

However, Israel's Channel 12 TV has launched an attack on Egypt's Al-Azhar Foundation and its Sheikh, accusing the foundation's schools of promoting hatred. The channel alleges that Al-Azhar's educational system, attended by two million students, instills a hostile attitude toward Israel and Jews, both locally and globally. Furthermore, the channel has claimed that the Grand Imam of Al-Azhar, Sheikh Ahmed Al-Tayeb, maintains connections with Hamas. In light of these accusations, scholarly analysis and dialogue are crucial to discern the complexities of religious and political narratives surrounding the Israeli-Palestinian conflict (MEM, 2024).

The rhetoric of these influential Arab scholars and jurists, particularly when disseminated to Muslim and immigrant communities, has contributed significantly to the inflamed climate of antisemitism. These figures have made statements that not only echo but also intensify existing antisemitic sentiments. For instance, speakers at a mosque in Fort Lauderdale, Florida, on April 20, 2024, likened Jews to a 'poison-injecting virus,' denying the Holocaust and accusing Mossad agents of orchestrating anti-Jewish violence.

Such inflammatory remarks not only propagate conspiracy theories but also dehumanize and demonize Jewish people, contributing to an environment of hostility and discrimination.

Moreover, the influence of these scholars extends beyond the local sphere, as demonstrated by Imam Tarik Ata's address to Muslim students in Orange County, California, on April 26, 2024. Ata's rhetoric, which promises divine reward for inflicting fear, anger, and pain on Jews, illustrates the dangerous intersection of religious zealotry and incitement to violence.

Similarly, the President of Tehran's Toosi University, Dr. Amir Reza Shahani, on April 30, 2024, extended an invitation to American students and professors expelled due to campus protests, suggesting a platform for the dissemination of extremist ideologies. These examples highlight the global reach of such rhetoric and its potential to radicalize individuals and communities, perpetuating antisemitic beliefs and violence.

In summary, the rhetoric of influential scholars in the Muslim world, infused with Jihadi ideology, has transformed antisemitism from mere hatred to a call for the annihilation of Jews worldwide. Figures such as Sheikh Othman Al-Khamis and Mustafa Al-Adawi have utilized their platforms to propagate inflammatory messages that incite violence and exacerbate tensions. This shift is evident in their endorsements of militant actions against Israel and their calls for widespread Jihad, which manipulate religious symbols and narratives to justify acts of aggression. For instance, Al-Adawi's invocation of religious duty to support Hamas through prayer, financial assistance, or armed struggle highlights a disturbing trend where religious rhetoric is weaponized to fuel antisemitic sentiments and violence.

This shift in rhetoric has had significant repercussions beyond the Middle East, sparking protests, boycotts, and social media activism across the Muslim world and extending to minority Muslim communities in the West. The October 7 attack on Israel and the subsequent Gaza conflict have catalyzed a wave of solidarity with Palestine and condemnation of Israeli actions.

Protests have erupted from Indonesia and Pakistan to the Middle East and North Africa, reflecting a unified stance against Israel's policies. This global groundswell of anger has led to boycott campaigns against Western brands perceived to have ties to Israel, with companies like McDonald's, Starbucks, and KFC facing backlash in countries such as Egypt, Jordan, Kuwait, and Morocco.

Economic antisemitism, characterized by prejudicial attitudes and discriminatory actions towards Jewish individuals or groups based on economic considerations, represents a notable facet of this ongoing situation. Throughout history, economic antisemitism has been employed to rationalize discriminatory policies and behaviors targeting Jewish communities. In the current context, the calls for boycotts and the targeting of Western brands echo historical patterns, demonstrating the enduring complexity of antisemitism in various societal contexts. The utilization of economic measures as a form of protest perceived injustices inflicted by Israel underscores how deeply entrenched antisemitic sentiments can manifest in contemporary movements.

Moreover, the shift among orthodox scholars from advocating Jihad against Shia regimes to endorsing pro-Iranian militias attacking Israel underscores the effectiveness of Iranian strategies in uniting Muslim communities against Israel. This convergence under the guise of liberating Al-Aqsa and eradicating Jews marks a troubling trend, where historical and ideological differences are set aside to focus on a common adversary.

The manipulation of religious fervor to garner support for militant actions not only perpetuates violence but also exposes the hypocrisy of leaders who incite conflict from safe havens while leaving vulnerable populations exposed to military actions. The endorsement of Jihad by influential scholars amplifies the call for annihilation and represents a dangerous escalation in the antisemitic narrative, with far-reaching implications for global security and interfaith relations.

In conclusion, addressing the transformation of antisemitism into a call for Israel's annihilation in the Muslim world requires a multifaceted approach. Education should emphasize tolerance and peaceful coexistence, countering radical interpretations of religious texts. Community engagement programs are crucial for fostering dialogue and empathy among diverse communities. Additionally, policymakers and international organizations must prioritize conflict resolution efforts that address the grievances of all parties involved in the Israeli-Palestinian conflict. By promoting understanding, dialogue, and peaceful resolution, we can combat antisemitism and extremist rhetoric, working towards a more inclusive and peaceful world.

2.4 Jihadist Ideologies and Antisemitism: The Trojan Horse Threat in Australia.

Australia, while grappling with the return of ISIS fighters and Jihadi brides, has confronted a series of terrorist attacks that underscore the evolving landscape of radicalism within the nation. The Holsworthy Barracks terror plot in August 2009 involved five individuals planning an Islamist terrorist attack on an Australian Army training area. These individuals, connected with the Somali-based terrorist group al-Shabaab, were apprehended and received lengthy prison sentences, with the judge noting their ongoing threat to society due to their unrepentant jihadist ideologies.

Similarly, the 2014 Endeavour Hills stabbings witnessed 18-year-old Numan Haider stabbing two counter-terrorism officers in Melbourne before being shot dead. These incidents highlight the transition from cognitive radicalism to weaponized and violent radicalism, where individuals like Haider pose significant threats due to their entrenched jihadist attitudes. The 2014 Sydney hostage crisis, orchestrated by Islamist Haron Monis, further exemplified the evolving threat of terrorism in Australia. Monis held hostages in a Lindt chocolate café in Sydney's Martin Place, resulting in tragic fatalities.

Additionally, the 2017 Brighton siege and the 2018 Melbourne stabbing attack underscore the persistent threat of terrorism within the country. These events reflect the potential for radicalized individuals to carry out violent acts, demonstrating a broader trend of radicalization and extremist ideology within Australia.

This trend is further exemplified by the rise of antisemitic incidents within Australia's Muslim communities, which has posed significant challenges to the country's security landscape. The intertwining of Islamist extremism with antisemitism, as seen in the transmission of ideologies from European far-right movements to Islamist factions, underscores the complex nature of radicalization in Australia. This convergence of radical ideologies has not only fueled antisemitic sentiments but also manifested in a surge of assaults and harassment against the Jewish community. These incidents emphasize the urgent need for comprehensive strategies to address radicalization and extremism in all its forms within Australian society.

In addition to these antisemitic incidents, extremism within Australian Muslim communities is significantly fueled by radical preachers who exploit the populace's limited religious knowledge. With language barriers and a lack of understanding of Arabic and Quranic sciences, many Muslims heavily rely on interpretations provided by their Imams and religious leaders. These preachers often selectively quote Quranic verses and Hadiths to present a distorted version of Islam that justifies violence and intolerance.

By manipulating religious texts, they construct a narrative of perpetual conflict, portraying the West as an inherent enemy of Islam. This portrayal suggests that true Muslims cannot integrate into Western societies, fostering an environment of fear, suspicion, and hostility towards non-Muslims. The preachers' strategic manipulation of religious texts serves to legitimize violent behavior and embolden extremist actions, effectively creating a framework within which radical ideologies can thrive.

The influence of these radical preachers stems not from their religious expertise but from their activism and militant stance. This allows them to attract followers, particularly among the youth, who may be more susceptible to radicalization. By positioning themselves as defenders of

Islam against a perceived Western threat, they exploit socio-political grievances and personal frustrations to galvanize support.

Their charismatic leadership and compelling narratives draw in individuals searching for identity and purpose, ultimately leading some towards violent extremism. The radical preachers' ability to disseminate their extremist ideology through community networks and social media platforms further amplifies their reach and impact. Consequently, their rhetoric and actions contribute to the broader radicalization process within Australian Muslim communities, posing significant challenges to social cohesion and national security.

For example, as early as 2014, Umm Abdullatif, an Australian Islamic State (ISIS) propagator, used social media to urge ISIS supporters to carry out attacks on Anzac Day, a significant day of remembrance. Similarly, Neil Prakash, an Australian ISIS operative and preacher, called on Australian Muslims to join ISIS and terrorize Australian communities.

These preachers manipulate religious teachings to justify violence, fostering a climate of radicalization. By distorting Quranic verses and Hadiths, they craft a narrative that glorifies martyrdom and violence against perceived enemies. This strategic manipulation of religious doctrine is instrumental in creating an environment conducive to extremism and terrorism, thereby posing a significant threat to societal harmony and security.

Furthermore, figures like Ismail Al-Wahwah and Imam Sufyaan Khalifa have propagated conspiracy theories, such as denying the Holocaust and alleging that global events like

9/11 and the COVID-19 pandemic are orchestrated by a Zionist conspiracy. These statements not only spread hate and intolerance but also contribute to radicalizing individuals and inciting violence against perceived enemies, particularly the Jewish community.

The dissemination of such conspiracy theories underscores the role of radical preachers in perpetuating antisemitism and fostering a mindset that legitimizes violent actions against Jews and other marginalized groups.

In the aftermath of the October 7 incident, several Australian Islamic scholars have come under scrutiny for their inflammatory rhetoric and incitement to violence within Western Muslim communities. Nassim Abdi, on October 10, 2023, controversially dismissed the concept of 'innocent victims' from the October 7 event, alleging that these individuals had provoked Palestinians and manipulated Western sympathy by selectively portraying only attractive female victims in revealing clothing.

Such statements not only dehumanize the victims but also rationalize violence by blaming the victims for their plight. Similarly, Brother Ismail, on October 27, 2023, voiced his support for Hamas and advocated for jihad as the solution for the Muslim nation. He equated the flags of ISIS and Al-Qaeda with the identity of the entire Muslim community, while chastising Sunnis for not engaging in actions against Israel akin to those of Iran.

In a lecture delivered on November 4, 2023, at the Al-Madina Dawah Centre, Wissam 'Abu Ousayd' Haddad espoused anti-Semitic rhetoric, characterizing Jews as vermin, lacking in courage, and wielding disproportionate influence over media and financial institutions. He rejected the distinction between Jews and Zionists, portraying them as a unified malevolent force and cautioning of their future antagonism towards Muslims.

Such rhetoric not only vilifies an entire community but also sows seeds of division and animosity. Similarly, Kamal Abu Mariam, in a sermon delivered on November 24, 2023, at the Sydney Roselands Mosque, urged a boycott of corporations supporting the 'Zionist criminal apartheid Nazi Regime', employing violent historical references and advocating for the annihilation of Jews. This incitement to economic and physical violence highlights the dangerous potential of radical sermons in mobilizing individuals towards extremist actions.

Furthermore, on December 1, 2023, Omar Najjarine delivered a sermon that perpetuated anti-Israel sentiments, suggesting that Jewish settlers in Muslim lands prefer governance under Islamic rule. He referenced Quranic verses warning about the Israelites' troublesome nature and questioned the rationale behind expectations from a group he claimed was cursed by Allah. These statements perpetuate historical prejudices and encourage hostility and violence against Jews, contributing to a cycle of hate and retaliation. This convergence of radical ideologies has fueled antisemitic sentiments and manifested in a surge of assaults and harassment against the Jewish community. These incidents underscore the urgent need for comprehensive strategies to address radicalization and extremism in all its forms within Australian society.

The presence of these radical Imams in Australia advocating for the killing of Jews, Jihad within the country, and the annihilation of Israel poses a significant threat to societal harmony and security. These preachers, through their inflammatory rhetoric, manipulate the youth and masses, instilling a sense of violence and terror. Such messages not only endanger the safety of Jewish communities but also disrupt the peaceful coexistence of diverse populations within Australia.

The radicalization process, which can escalate from cognitive acceptance of extremist ideologies to structured planning and ultimately to terrorism, underscores the urgency of addressing the influence of these preachers. Their teachings have the potential to radicalize individuals swiftly, leading to the commission of acts of violence and terror, and thus, necessitate a comprehensive strategy to counter radicalization and uphold societal cohesion.

Most of these radical preachers, advocating for violence and extremism within Australia, are non-Australian citizens or descendants of immigrants. They represent a Trojan horse of Jihadism that has infiltrated various Muslim communities across the country, exploiting the ongoing geopolitical conflict involving Israel to intimidate and threaten local Jewish populations.

Despite their pervasive influence and disruptive agendas, Australian authorities have largely skirted around this issue for decades, failing to effectively confront and dismantle this extremist network. Policymakers and relevant institutions must implement more stringent measures to counter this threat, prioritizing concrete actions over political rhetoric and theoretical discussions.

Worse, the infiltration of foreign radical preachers into Australia poses a significant threat to its safety and security, representing yet another facet of this Trojan Horse of Jihadism. These preachers often conduct workshops in Australia, both physically and virtually, leveraging their English fluency and existing popularity in countries like the US, Canada, and the UK. Hosted by local Salafi scholars, they propagate their ideologies to capture a wide audience, highlighting vulnerabilities in Australia's immigration laws, online surveillance, and policymaking.

For instance, in 2013, Abu Adnan, a hardline Sydney Islamic preacher, hosted Bilal Philips, a notorious scholar with millions of followers, despite Philips being denied an Australian entry visa in 2007 due to national security concerns. This incident underscores the ease with which radical scholars can exploit loopholes and spread divisive narratives, such as Abu Adnan's criticism of Muslims supporting the Australian government as 'House Negros,' creating an 'Us versus them' mentality.

Additionally, workshops conducted by figures like Bilal Philips, Khalid Yasin, and Siraj Wahhaj in New Zealand, which were criticized for allegedly inciting Jihad against Jews and Christians, underscore the necessity for stricter measures to counter such influences.

Moreover, the online presence of Salafi scholars like Sheikh Assim al-Hakeem further exacerbates the issue. Al-Hakeem advocates for extreme measures, including the execution of ex-Muslims and equating apostasy with treason. In 2020, he condemned the efforts of Australian Imam Muhammad Tawhidi, known as the 'Imam of peace,' labeling him as an intelligence agent used to infiltrate Muslim communities in Australia.

Similarly, Abu Usamah At-Thahabi, another preacher with a strong online following in Australia, has praised Osama bin Laden and advocated for Jihad against Jews, Christians, and homosexuals. These examples, just a drop in the ocean, underscore the urgent need for Australia to address the proliferation of radical preachers and their dangerous ideologies, implementing more robust measures to safeguard against extremist influences and protect its diverse communities.

In conclusion, the proliferation of radical preachers within Australia's vastly growing Muslim communities, encompassing diverse ethnicities such as Somalian, East-Asian, and Arab populations, has the potential to cultivate a hostile environment. This environment threatens the safety and security not only of Jewish communities but of Australians as a whole. It appears as a mini-Middle East is being established within Australia, creating a state of chaos within a democratic framework.

This phenomenon has been observed in the violent pro-Palestinian protests and is likely to continue amid the ongoing Israeli conflict. There is a fear that Iran may exploit this radical atmosphere in Australia to unify Shia and Sunni communities, organizing and arming them, similar to Iran's strategy in Gaza, under the guise of liberating Al-Aqsa. Consequently, antisemitism based on hatred may escalate to the effective annihilation of Jews within Australia, given the prevailing sentiments and slogans supporting such actions.

Hence, Australian authorities and relevant intelligence agencies must urgently acknowledge the gravity of the situation posed by the proliferation of radical preachers and the potential for hostile environments within the country. To effectively address this threat, they must employ a multifaceted approach that combines both soft and hard measures.

Soft measures should include proactive community engagement and education to counter extremist ideologies and promote social cohesion. Hard measures should involve robust enforcement of existing laws and regulations, enhanced surveillance of radical elements, and stringent border control to prevent the entry of extremist individuals. Only through a comprehensive strategy that addresses the root causes and manifestations of radicalization can Australia hope to safeguard its diverse communities and protect its national security.

Chapter Two Conclusion.

The ongoing existential conflict between Israel and surrounding hostile militias has profound and far-reaching implications for Jewish communities globally, including those in Australia. As Israel grapples with relentless threats to its security, Jewish communities abroad are increasingly targeted as scapegoats, suffering a resurgence of antisemitism fueled by the geopolitical turmoil.

This surge in antisemitism is not merely a byproduct of regional hostilities but a manifestation of deep-seated prejudices that have been reignited in the wake of the conflict. Jewish individuals and institutions in the West find themselves under siege, facing heightened discrimination and violence as they are unjustly held accountable for actions and policies of the Israeli state.

The impact of this conflict extends beyond physical and psychological safety, affecting the social and political standing of Jewish communities. In Australia, as in other Western countries, there has been a noticeable rise in antisemitic incidents, from verbal abuse and vandalism to more organized forms of hatred and exclusion.

This surge in antisemitism is particularly alarming as it has evolved into calls for the annihilation of Jews, further intensifying the climate of fear and hostility. Such extreme rhetoric not only jeopardizes the well-being of Jewish individuals but also undermines the fabric of multicultural societies by promoting division and intolerance.

This troubling trend underscores the broader societal repercussions of the Israeli-Palestinian conflict, where Jewish communities worldwide bear the brunt of ancient biases reawakened by modern strife. As the conflict continues unabated, the need for robust measures to protect and support Jewish communities in the diaspora becomes ever more critical, highlighting the interconnectedness of global Jewish security and the stability of the Middle East.

To effectively eradicate antisemitism in Australia, it is imperative for communities, organizations, and government agencies to collaborate on comprehensive education programs, enforce strict legal measures against hate crimes, and promote interfaith dialogue to foster mutual understanding and respect.

Chapter Three

Antisemitism in Limbo:

Political Accusations and Academic Controversies

Introduction.

The landscape of antisemitism in Australia is marked by a complex state of limbo, where efforts to combat genuine hatred and prejudice against Jews juggle precariously with the preservation of free expression, political critique, and academic freedom. This chapter delves into the intricate dynamics that have surfaced in recent years, focusing on the political and academic discourse surrounding antisemitism.

Former Prime Minister Scott Morrison played a pivotal role in shaping Australia's policy towards antisemitism and Israel. His recognition of West Jerusalem as the capital of Israel, the adoption of the International Holocaust Remembrance Alliance (IHRA) working definition of antisemitism, and his condemnation of antisemitic rhetoric at the United Nations exemplify his strong stance. Morrison's unwavering support for Israel has been both lauded and criticized, reflecting broader tensions within Australia's political sphere.

The 2022 Federal Election, which brought Anthony Albanese to power, introduced a new phase of political discourse. Albanese's nuanced views on the Israeli-Palestinian conflict, including his advocacy for Palestinian rights and commitment to a two-state solution, signal a departure from Morrison's policies and raise concerns within the Australian Jewish community. These political shifts highlight the ongoing juggling act between addressing antisemitic rhetoric and maintaining diplomatic and political balance.

Furthermore, the chapter addresses the academic controversies that have emerged around antisemitism, highlighting critiques from political figures like Julia Gillard and Peter Dutton, and the challenges of balancing criticism of Israel with combating antisemitic rhetoric and violence. These debates underscore the state of limbo in which antisemitism currently resides, caught between political accusations and scholarly disputes. By exploring these political and academic debates, this chapter provides a comprehensive overview of the current state of antisemitism in Australia and the multifaceted challenges it poses.

3.1 Contested Antisemitism: The Australian Debate and the Criticism of Israel.

The International Holocaust Remembrance Alliance (IHRA) definition of antisemitism has been widely embraced by governments and institutions worldwide, including the United States, Canada, and the European Union. Meticulously crafted by an international panel of experts, this definition provides a comprehensive framework for identifying and combating antisemitism, fostering tolerance, understanding, and respect among all communities. It includes illustrative examples that reveal how anti-Israel rhetoric can conceal antisemitism, such as substituting 'Israeli' or 'Zionist' for 'Jew' in conspiratorial stereotypes.

However, the IHRA definition has sparked controversy within the Jewish community. While it offers a clear understanding of antisemitic behavior and addresses harmful perceptions of

Jews, critics argue it has been misused to stifle legitimate criticism of Israel and suppress free speech, leading to a state of limbo regarding the concept of antisemitism.

The Boycott, Divestment, Sanctions (BDS) movement exemplifies the challenges in distinguishing political critique from antisemitic rhetoric. BDS advocates contest accusations of antisemitism, arguing their actions constitute political protest rather than expressions of hatred towards Jews. This debate highlights the delicate balance required to address antisemitism without infringing on legitimate political discourse.

Australia's membership in the IHRA on June 4, 2019, marked a significant milestone in its commitment to combating antisemitism and promoting Holocaust remembrance. Prompted by rising intimidation, harassment, and online hate targeting Australian Jews, major Jewish organizations have advocated for the adoption of the IHRA definition, emphasizing that Jewish people, as the primary victims of antisemitism, should define it. Just as only those who suffer from an ailment can truly describe its pain and intensity, it is those who experience antisemitism who can best articulate its manifestations and impacts.

This move would empower institutions like anti-discrimination bodies, law enforcement, media, education, and sports organizations to incorporate the definition into their operations, facilitating the identification and addressing of antisemitism (AIJAC, 2021).

Despite its significance, the IHRA definition is contentious. Organizations like the Australia/Israel & Jewish Affairs

Council and the Zionist Federation of Australia endorse it for its educational value, promoting a nuanced understanding of antisemitism.

However, groups such as the New Israel Fund Australia and the Australia Palestine Advocacy Network worry that it conflates antisemitism with criticism of Israel, potentially stifling legitimate discourse and advocacy for Palestine. Liam Getreu of the New Israel Fund Australia notes that this conflation, exemplified by the Trump administration's use of the definition, complicates efforts to identify and confront genuine antisemitism (Doherty, 2021).

In light of these debates, the adoption of the IHRA definition by various Australian councils, states, and political organizations marks a significant milestone in combating racism and antisemitism. Waverley Council's adoption, timed with Chanukah, demonstrates a commitment to its Jewish community, highlighting the definition's role in informing strategic plans and actions (Media Release, 2021).

New South Wales, the first Australian state to adopt the IHRA definition following Premier Dominic Perrottet's announcement, aligns with the federal government's earlier adoption, emphasizing the need for a clear definition to combat antisemitism effectively.

The Jewish-Australian organization Anti-Defamation Commission, represented by Dvir Abramovich, supports expanding the definition to protect Jewish students' rights and advocates for similar legislation in Australia (JNS, 2021). Victoria's adoption of the IHRA definition by the Andrews

Labor Government reinforces this commitment, providing a framework for understanding and combating antisemitism.

The Jewish Council of Australia, led by Max Kaiser, emphasizes the importance of providing diverse Jewish perspectives in media and community discourse. South Australia's Legislative Council's adoption of the IHRA definition, spearheaded by One Nation MLC Sarah Game, underscores the importance of recognizing and combating antisemitism (Kelsall, 2022).

The adoption of the IHRA definition by Australian Young Labor reflects a broader recognition of the need to combat antisemitism and promote inclusivity on university campuses. Alissa Foster, president of the Australasian Union of Jewish Students (AUJS), welcomed the decision for its potential to create a more comfortable environment for Jewish students.

Leaders from the Executive Council of Australian Jewry (ECAJ) and the Zionist Federation of Australia praised the resolution, aligning Young Labor's policy with the broader Labor Party and Prime Minister Albanese's views (Kohn, 2023). This widespread support for the IHRA definition underscores the critical need for a nuanced understanding of antisemitism, as highlighted by scholars and experts in the field.

Jamie Hyams, a senior policy analyst at the Australia/Israel & Jewish Affairs Council, underscores the critical importance of accurately understanding antisemitism, advocating for the IHRA definition as the most authoritative framework developed by an international panel of experts. Addressing critics such as Michael Bradley, who contend that the definition politicizes antisemitism and constrains academic freedom, Hyams argues that the definition merely restricts the freedom to perpetuate racism, a limitation he deems necessary and justifiable beyond the scope of academic freedom.

He suggests that individuals who feel constrained by the definition should introspect on the reasons behind their disproportionately harsh criticism of Israel, implying that such criticism may be indicative of underlying antisemitic biases (Hyams, 2023).

Hyams further elucidates that contemporary antisemites frequently disguise their antisemitism as criticism of Israel. The IHRA definition incorporates examples to address these modern manifestations. He clarifies that these examples are not inherently categorized as antisemitic but are context dependent. Instances such as denying Jews the right to self-determination or equating Israeli policies with those of the Nazis are highlighted as potential forms of antisemitism, as they can serve to delegitimize Israel and foment hatred towards Jews.

Additionally, Hyams corrects the common misconception that Kenneth Stern was the 'lead drafter' of the definition, clarifying that Stern's involvement was limited. He emphasizes the contributions of other key drafters, including Rabbi Andrew Baker, Deidre Berger, and Michael Whine, who view the definition as vital in the fight against antisemitism.

By addressing contemporary manifestations of antisemitism, such as the misuse of criticism of Israel and Zionism, and clarifying the nuanced approach of the IHRA definition, Hyams contributes to a more nuanced understanding of antisemitism and the measures needed to combat it effectively, highlighting the importance of distinguishing between legitimate criticism of Israeli policies and antisemitic rhetoric.

This nuanced approach is echoed by other scholars and experts in the field, as the discourse surrounding the intersection of anti-Zionism and antisemitism is characterized by a complex array of perspectives. Professor Greg Rose of the University of Wollongong posits that Zionism is inherently linked to Judaism, arguing that while the IHRA definition of antisemitism is not legally binding, it provides a valuable framework for understanding and addressing antisemitism.

However, Dr. Suzanne Rutland, a member of the IHRA, acknowledges the controversy surrounding certain IHRA examples, particularly those linking criticism of Israel or Zionism with antisemitism, suggesting the need for a nuanced approach. Dr. Rutland emphasizes the distinction between legitimate criticism of Israeli policies and the denial of Israel's right to exist, cautioning against equating Israel with apartheid or evil, as this can lead to abuse against diaspora Jews.

Building on these perspectives, Max Kaiser from the Jewish Council of Australia highlights the diverse political perspectives within the Australian Jewish community, noting groups such as the Loud Jew Collective and Tzedek that advocate non-Zionist or anti-Zionist viewpoints. He emphasizes the importance of distinguishing between antisemitism and anti-Zionism, advocating for the Jerusalem Declaration as a clearer alternative to the IHRA definition.

David Slucki, director of the Australian Centre for Jewish Civilization at Monash University, delves into the nuances of anti-Zionism and antisemitism, acknowledging the potential overlap while asserting that criticism of Israel is not inherently antisemitic. He raises concerns about the rise of neo-Nazism in Australia and emphasizes the need for empathy and understanding within the Jewish community regarding diverse views on Zionism. Dr. Slucki's insights underscore the complexity of the issue and the importance of nuanced discussions to address antisemitic rhetoric effectively (Marin, 2024).

Transitioning from these academic insights, it is evident that despite the adoption of the IHRA definition of antisemitism by various governments and organizations, Jewish communities continue to face significant discrimination and threats. The European Union Agency for Fundamental Rights (FRA) survey among Jewish Europeans indicates that the examples in the definition align with the experiences of the victims.

However, the adoption of the IHRA definition has been complex and contentious, with debates on its implications for free speech, potential politicization, and effectiveness in combating antisemitism. While the definition provides a framework for understanding antisemitism, it has not necessarily reduced incidents or improved responses to the challenges faced by Jewish communities. Therefore, a comprehensive approach, including education, legislation, and a commitment to fighting all forms of hatred and discrimination, is essential to effectively address antisemitic rhetoric and violence.

In conclusion, the adoption of the IHRA definition of antisemitism by various Australian councils, states, and political organizations is a significant step towards combating antisemitism and promoting Holocaust remembrance. While the definition has been contested by anti-Israel and anti-Zionist entities, its adoption demonstrates a commitment to combating antisemitic rhetoric and violence. The IHRA definition provides a clear framework for identifying and combating antisemitism, and it also enhances Australia's foreign policy and diplomacy with Israel.

By endorsing the definition, which acknowledges that criticism of Israel, when similar in nature to critiques of other nations, should not be labeled as antisemitic, the Australian government signals its respect for the Jewish people's right to self-determination. Promoting the IHRA definition and its importance can be achieved through education, awareness campaigns, and policies that promote tolerance, understanding, and respect for all communities.

3.2 Juggling Antisemitism: Balancing Academic Freedom and Jewish Rights in Australia.

Australian universities find themselves at the center of a contentious debate surrounding the adoption of the IHRA definition of antisemitism. This issue has sparked intense discussions and garnered both praise and criticism from various stakeholders. Despite mounting pressure from parliamentary MPs and the efforts of the Parliamentary Friends of IHRA, led by prominent figures such as Josh Burns, Allegra Spender, and Julian Leeser, some institutions have hesitated to embrace the definition unequivocally.

This hesitation is particularly striking given the prevalence of conspiracy theories propagated by Australian radical preachers such as Ismail Al-Wahwah and Sufyaan Khalifa, who have denied the Holocaust and promoted anti-Jewish sentiments, including allegations that global events like 9/11 and the COVID-19 pandemic are orchestrated by Israeli Zionists.

In contrast, other universities, such as the University of Melbourne, have adopted the IHRA definition, garnering praise from Jewish organizations like the Zionist Federation of Australia (ZFA) and the Australia/Israel & Jewish Affairs Council (AIJAC). However, this decision has also faced criticism from Palestinian advocacy groups, such as the Australian Palestine Advocacy Network (APAN), who argue that the definition conflates antisemitism with anti-Zionism and assert that Israel's policies towards Palestinians should be open to scrutiny.

The debate continues to unfold, with some universities like the University of Adelaide opting not to adopt the definition, citing their commitment to cultural diversity, critical thinking, and respectful debate. Meanwhile, others, such as the University of Sydney, are considering its implementation as part of their anti-racist efforts (Soit, 2023).

The University of Melbourne has emerged as a leader in this regard, having adopted the IHRA definition as part of its commitment to fostering a welcoming and safe environment for all community members. This decision has been praised by Jewish organizations such as the ZFA and the AIJAC, who view it as a crucial step in combating antisemitism and promoting understanding. The move by the University of Melbourne is particularly significant considering offensive motions passed by the university's student union, underscoring the urgent need for a clear definition of antisemitism to guide educational efforts and combat discrimination.

The Australasian Union of Jewish Students (AUJS) has repeatedly criticized the University of Melbourne Student Union (UMSU) for its contentious positions on Israel and Zionism. In August 2022, UMSU endorsed the global BDS campaign, accusing Israel of 'massacres, forced expulsion, and genocide,' and labeling Zionism as 'racist and colonial.' This move drew widespread condemnation from prominent Zionist and Jewish organizations in Australia, including the Australia/Israel and Jewish Affairs Council and the Executive Council of Australian Jewry, who argued that it exacerbates campus hostility towards Jewish students without aiding Palestinians.

In February 2024, UMSU rescinded the controversial anti-Israel motion in response to a legal challenge, resulting in the union retracting the motion and covering the legal costs. AUJS president Noah Loven praised the settlement as a positive step towards reconciliation, highlighting improved relations with the new UMSU executive and a surge in AUJS memberships, indicating Jewish students' need for solidarity in a challenging campus environment.

This development has sparked a broader discussion about the need for concrete actions to support Jewish Australians. Dr. Dvir Abramovich welcomed the decision and emphasized the critical importance of protecting students from antisemitism. Abramovich advocates for the expanded definition of antisemitism to safeguard the rights of Jewish students and calls for similar legislation in Australia. However, Max Kaiser expresses apprehension regarding the legislation, fearing it may impede legitimate political expression and peaceful protests, particularly regarding the Israeli-Palestinian conflict. Kaiser argues that existing laws already provide protection against antisemitic discrimination and cautions against equating criticism of Israel with antisemitism (Carr, 2024).

Despite the University of Melbourne's proactive stance, the adoption of the IHRA definition remains a subject of debate at other Australian universities. While Macquarie University and the University of Wollongong have embraced the definition, others, such as the University of Sydney, are still deliberating its implementation. Concerns about the legal implications and potential limitations of the definition have been raised by the University of New South Wales and Griffith University, with the latter deciding against adoption. James Cook University and the University of Queensland, on the other hand, believe that their existing policies may suffice in addressing antisemitism on campus.

The controversy surrounding the IHRA definition has not been limited to academic circles, as political advocacy groups like Boycott Divestment and Sanctions Australia have criticized the Parliamentary Friends of IHRA for potentially breaching rules about political neutrality. Despite these challenges, the Zionist Federation of Australia continues to advocate for the IHRA definition's wider adoption as a critical tool in combating the growing threat of antisemitism.

This ongoing debate underscores the complex nature of balancing academic freedom with the need to address antisemitism effectively, highlighting the importance of open dialogue and collaboration in finding meaningful solutions to these pressing issues.

Amidst this broader national debate, the University of Adelaide's decision not to adopt the IHRA Working Definition of Antisemitism, despite consulting with its Academic Board, reflects its commitment to principles of cultural diversity, critical thinking, and respectful debate. By emphasizing the importance of freedom of speech for democracy and academic freedom, the university has chosen to adopt the Model Code on freedom of speech recommended by Robert French.

This approach is designed to ensure that all members of the university community feel safe from discrimination and persecution, while condemning antisemitism as a form of bigotry. The university reaffirms its commitment to fair and non-discriminatory treatment for both staff and students (Adelaide, 2023).

In contrast, La Trobe University has adopted the IHRA definition but has excluded its 11 examples, citing concerns that these examples could potentially restrict academic freedom and reasonable political debate, particularly regarding Israel. Alongside the IHRA definition, La Trobe has also adopted the Jerusalem Declaration on Antisemitism (JDA) guidelines, which condemn antisemitism while supporting academic freedom.

This decision, influenced by Jewish advocacy groups and similar to the approach of Goldsmiths College at the University of London, seeks to strike a balance between condemning antisemitism and preserving academic freedom.

Vice-Chancellor John Dewar of La Trobe University has emphasized the institution's commitment to condemning antisemitism, supporting victims, preserving free speech, and developing an anti-racism strategy (Visontay, 2023). However, the ZFA, led by President Jeremy Leibler, has expressed significant concern over La Trobe's partial adoption of the IHRA definition and its use of the JDA. Leibler cited a survey revealing that 73% of Jewish students at La Trobe conceal their identity due to antisemitism, criticizing the university for consulting fringe groups without engaging major Jewish organizations or the AUJS (ZFA, 2023).

As the University of Adelaide's Council deliberates on the IHRA definition, another Australian institution is embroiled in a heated debate over the same issue. The University of Sydney's Academic Standards and Policy Committee (ASPC) has proposed a motion to the Academic Board to adopt the IHRA definition as part of its anti-racist efforts.

This proposal has sparked intense debate, with USyd Students' Representative Council President Lia Perkins supporting the initiative but expressing concerns that the focus on the IHRA definition may overshadow the Palestinian struggle. NTEU President Dr. Nick Riemer opposes the endorsement, arguing that the IHRA definition suppresses legitimate criticism of Israel and urging the University to prioritize academic freedom.

In a striking irony, just as the University of Sydney is grappling with the IHRA definition, a group of students and external protesters has been camping out at the University, demanding that all academic ties with Israel be severed. Families for Palestine expressed support for these actions, calling the students 'courageous' in an Instagram post.

The situation escalated when videos surfaced of young children chanting for an intifada during a pro-Palestinian protest at USYD, with chants in Arabic calling Israel 'haram' and a small girl chanting, "from the river to the sea, Palestine will be free." This antisemitic rhetoric was accompanied by chants of "5, 6, 7, 8, Israel is a terrorist state" and accusations against Prime Minister Albanese of supporting genocide. The group also called for divestment from what they termed 'Apartheid Israel' (Ganko, 2024).

Despite the eventual suspension of the pro-Palestinian students for disrupting classes, the Executive Council of Australian Jewry's co-chief executive, Peter Wertheim, criticized the response as "far too little and far too late." He highlighted the disruptive impact of the protesters' actions on classes and the pervasive atmosphere of fear and anxiety created among students and staff (White, 2024).

Grenier, a Jewish student, also pointed out the university's failure to protect Jewish students, noting that "more than half of Jewish students are reported hiding their faith, removing religious clothing, and avoiding class to escape harassment." The University of Sydney's ongoing inability to address serious antisemitism and protect Jewish students is a pressing issue that requires immediate and decisive action.

In conclusion, the adoption of the IHRA Working Definition of Antisemitism in Australia represents a pivotal measure in combating antisemitic rhetoric and safeguarding Jewish rights, despite the presence of alternative frameworks like the Jerusalem Declaration on Antisemitism. This definition offers a clear and comprehensive approach to identifying and addressing antisemitism, ensuring that academic institutions do not become safe havens for hate speech disguised as political critique. The ongoing debates and challenges surrounding its adoption underscore the complex juggling act between academic freedom and the necessity of addressing antisemitic rhetoric.

The surge in antisemitic incidents and violent pro-Palestinian protests on Australian campuses highlights the need for a multifaceted approach. This involves collaboration between policymakers, university leaders, and security agencies to implement strict measures that protect Jewish students while upholding the values of academic freedom and respectful dialogue. Through decisive action, including the unequivocal adoption of the IHRA definition and enhanced education and awareness programs, Australia can effectively safeguard its Jewish communities while maintaining robust academic discourse.

3.3 A Stand for Jewish Rights: Leadership Against Antisemitism in Australia.

In recent years, the political landscape has seen a marked increase in the awareness and condemnation of antisemitism, with leaders around the world taking definitive stands against this age-old hatred. In Australia, Julia Gillard, Scott Morrison, and Peter Dutton have emerged as notable figures in this fight, demonstrating a steadfast commitment to Jewish rights and setting a precedent for political leadership against antisemitism. This section delves into their political tenures, examining their policies, public statements, and community engagements that collectively underscore their resolve to combat antisemitic rhetoric and violence in Australia.

Julia Gillard.

Julia Gillard, Australia's first female Prime Minister, has been a prominent advocate against antisemitism and hate speech, offering valuable contributions and perspectives that provide significant historical context to the ongoing fight against antisemitism in Australia. Her involvement underscores the bipartisan nature of this issue, evidenced by her collaboration with other former Prime Ministers.

Her personal insights and public statements highlight the role of social media in distorting history and creating unbalanced views about the Israel-Hamas conflict, adding depth to the discourse. Furthermore, her criticisms of the government's handling of antisemitism and her calls for better policies emphasize the importance of governmental action and leadership in addressing this age-old prejudice.

Gillard has criticized the government's inadequate response to antisemitism, stating it "took longer than it should have" for people to decry the sexual violence used as a weapon of war during the October 7 attacks. She has emphasized the need for better education about the facts of the Israel-Hamas conflict and the pathways to peace, urging every Australian to call out antisemitism whenever they see it. The former Labor prime minister has also been critical of the government's handling of the conflict, arguing it has failed to provide adequate support for Israel and has instead focused on placating the progressive left.

These criticisms of the government's handling of the conflict and the need for better education on the issue have not been without controversy. Gillard has faced allegations that her pro-Israel stance is influenced by her partner Tim Mathieson's employment with Albert Dadon, a prominent supporter of Israel. These claims, made by former Australian ambassador to Israel Ross Burns, have been refuted by Gillard, who maintains that her views on Israel were established independently and publicly prior to Mathieson's employment.

Despite these allegations, Gillard has received support from Jewish leaders such as John Searle and Isi Leibler, who have praised her commitment to Israel and her call for an Israeli settlement freeze in Palestinian territories. Gillard's stance on Israel has been criticized by some Christian groups due to her atheism, but she has maintained that she will not pretend a faith she does not feel.

A significant example of the political accusations and conspiracy theories faced by Julia Gillard upon replacing

Kevin Rudd as Prime Minister demonstrates how antisemitism can be used to exploit public issues. Despite conspiracy theorists branding Rabbi Rudd as the political shift triggered unfounded antisemitic conspiracy theories from the far left, far right, and extremist Muslims, who falsely claimed a hidden Jewish influence in the transition.

This scenario underscores the persistent challenge of antisemitism infiltrating public discourse, diverting attention from genuine political analysis to baseless and harmful accusations. Gillard's experience highlights the need for a focused and rational approach to political criticism, free from the taint of antisemitic rhetoric.

Despite controversies and allegations regarding her stance on Israel, Julia Gillard has remained unwavering in her commitment to fight antisemitism. This is evidenced by her signing of the London Declaration on Combating Antisemitism, an action she took in Sydney alongside Jewish leaders. The declaration acknowledges the persistence of antisemitism despite significant historical milestones such as the end of World War II and the establishment of the State of Israel.

Gillard emphasized that antisemitism 'pollutes our world' and asserted that 'in the face of antisemitism, there can be no bystanders.' Her commitment was further reinforced by the support of at least 50 Australian lawmakers, including Tony Abbott, who also signed the declaration. While some critics argue that accusations of antisemitism are used to suppress criticism of Israel's policies, Gillard's dedication to combating this form of bigotry is clear and resolute.

Gillard's personal experiences with prejudice and her steadfast commitment to combating bigotry and intolerance underscore her dedication to addressing the persistent rise of antisemitism in Australia. In a Sky News Australia documentary presented by former treasurer Josh Frydenberg, Gillard shared her own experiences with prejudice and expressed her deep disturbance at recent incidents targeting the Jewish community.

These incidents included demonstrators chanting 'F*** Israel,' vandalizing schools with death threats, and expressing support for Hamas. Her public condemnation of these acts highlights her firm stance against antisemitism and her advocacy for the protection of Jewish Australians.

Julia Gillard has also emphasized the crucial role of museums in countering hate and fostering understanding. In a speech at the Jewish Museum of Australia, she underscored the importance of these institutions in promoting dialogue and combating antisemitism, asserting that 'places of truth-telling and remembrance never matter more than in the darkest of times.' Gillard highlighted the essential role museums play in addressing complex issues like colonialism and power imbalances.

In the documentary 'Never Again: The Fight Against Antisemitism,' she expressed deep concern over the rise of antisemitism in Australia following the October 7 attacks, describing prejudice as 'wholly repugnant' and criticizing social media for spreading 'misinformation' about the Israel-Hamas conflict, which has led to historical distortions and unbalanced views, particularly among young people.

Gillard's commitment to combating antisemitism is further demonstrated by her participation in a joint letter condemning the 'hatred' propagated by Hamas and expressing solidarity with Jewish Australians. The letter, drafted by Malcolm Turnbull, emphasized that 'there is no more tenaciously evil race hatred than antisemitism' and cautioned that Hamas aims to incite ancient hatreds worldwide.

The former prime ministers advocated for Israel to avoid civilian casualties and supported a two-state solution between Israel and Palestine, serving as a crucial reminder of the importance of promoting understanding and tolerance in the face of conflict. Her involvement, alongside other prominent political figures, highlights the bipartisan nature of this cause and the need for a unified stance against antisemitism in Australia.

In summary, Julia Gillard has been a vocal advocate against antisemitism, highlighting the importance of combating hate speech and promoting understanding and tolerance. Her involvement, alongside other former Prime Ministers, underscores the bipartisan nature of this fight, reflecting a national imperative that transcends political divides. Gillard's personal insights and public statements add depth to the discourse, criticizing the government's handling of related issues and emphasizing the crucial role of leadership in addressing antisemitic rhetoric.

Scott Morrison.

Former Prime Minister Scott Morrison, in a manner reminiscent of Julia Gillard, has demonstrated a steadfast commitment to combating antisemitism and supporting Israel in international forums. His unwavering stance is evident through several key events and decisions that have significantly influenced Australia's foreign policy.

In 2018, Morrison recognized West Jerusalem as the capital of Israel, acknowledging its status as the seat of the Knesset and other governmental institutions. This decision reaffirmed Australia's commitment to a two-state solution while criticizing the United Nations for its perceived antisemitic agenda and bias against Israel. Morrison's statement also recognized the Palestinian aspirations for a future state with its capital in East Jerusalem, reflecting Australia's commitment to a peaceful resolution of the Israeli-Palestinian conflict (Clench, 2018).

Despite criticism from the opposition, Morrison's decision received widespread support from the Jewish community. The Executive Council of Australian Jewry (ECAJ) praised the move as a recognition of reality, appreciating Morrison's critique of the United Nations' bias against Israel. The Israeli foreign ministry also welcomed the decision, viewing the opening of a trade and defense office in Jerusalem as a positive step.

Morrison further solidified his stance on the Israel-Palestine issue by criticizing NSW Labor leader Luke Foley for what he deemed 'antisemitic behavior' towards Vic Alhadeff, the chief executive of the NSW Jewish Board of Deputies (Tillet, 2018).

In November 2019, Morrison received the Jerusalem Prize, further cementing his strong stance against antisemitism. During the ceremony, he condemned the United Nations for allowing antisemitic sentiments to infiltrate its proceedings under the guise of human rights. This stance was commended by ZFA president Jeremy Leibler, who praised Morrison's opposition to 'anti-Israel resolutions' at the UN. Morrison acknowledged the global rise in antisemitism and reaffirmed Australia's commitment to Israel, emphasizing his duty to combat antisemitism.

On September 21, 2021, during the United Nations General Assembly, Morrison announced Australia's adoption of the IHRA working definition of antisemitism. This move was praised by Jeremy Leibler, who emphasized the importance of education in combating antisemitism. Minister for Education and Youth Alan Tudge supported the decision, noting its role in identifying and rejecting antisemitism, particularly on university campuses. This endorsement was described by Dvir Abramovich, chairman of the Anti-Defamation League, as a defeat for "Hitler and his modern-day guards of Auschwitz" (Harris, 2021).

The 2022 Federal Election brought a significant shift in leadership with Anthony Albanese's victory over Scott Morrison. Albanese, known for his criticism of Israel's policies and strong advocacy for Palestinian rights, has pledged continued friendship and support for Israel while affirming a commitment to a two-state solution and recognizing Palestine as a state, subject to future decisions by his government. This shift raised concerns within the Australian Jewish community regarding potential challenges to Israel-related policies.

Despite these concerns, Israeli Prime Minister Naftali Bennett expressed hope for deepening ties between Israel and Australia under Albanese's leadership. However, there are apprehensions about the potential decline in bipartisan support for Israel in Australia, with pro-Israel figures like former ambassador Dave Sharma and treasurer Josh Frydenberg being voted out of office.

The future of Australia's relationship with Israel and its stance on Palestinian rights remains a subject of scrutiny and debate, with the new Labor government's nuanced views marking a departure from Morrison's stance (Hoffman, 2022).

Following the October 7 terror attacks, Scott Morrison, who traveled to southern Israel with former British Prime Minister Boris Johnson, identified various forms of antisemitism and emphasized the need to stand in solidarity with the Jewish community. He apologized to Jewish attendees for their experiences of isolation, abandonment, persecution, threats, and hatred within Australia (Amy, 2024).

Additionally, Simon Birmingham, the Coalition's foreign affairs spokesperson, reiterated support for Israel's actions in Gaza while stressing the importance of caution in military operations and raising concerns about the UN agency UNRWA's alleged involvement in the October 7 attacks and history of fostering extremist views (Begley, 2024).

Former Prime Ministers Scott Morrison and Tony Abbott criticized Australia's decision to support a United Nations resolution allowing Palestine to join the United Nations, arguing that it 'rewards terrorists.' Abbott emphasized that recognition of Palestine should only occur when it can function as a state not governed by terrorist factions, while Morrison expressed concern that the vote could further isolate Jewish Australians amid rising antisemitism following the October 7 attacks. This criticism reflects a broader sentiment within the Liberal Party regarding the complexities of the Israel-Palestine conflict (Collins, 2024).

On the other hand, Professor Jeremy Salt critiques former Prime Ministers Scott Morrison and Julia Gillard for their stance on the Israel-Palestine conflict. While acknowledging Gillard's multiple visits to Israel and her post-political career focused on women's and children's rights, Salt argues that she failed to speak out against Israel's actions towards Palestinian women and children.

Similarly, Salt's criticism of Morrison overlooks his strong stance against antisemitism and his commitment to the Australia-Israel relationship, particularly in the wake of the October 7 attacks. Despite their efforts to navigate the complex geopolitical issues, the actions of both Morrison and Gillard have been misunderstood and misrepresented, highlighting the challenges faced by Australian politicians in addressing the Israel-Palestine conflict (Salt, 2024).

In Sum, Morrison's stance against antisemitism reflects the 'existential threat' paradigm, which suggests that the Jewish state is constantly under threat from antisemitic forces. This view is prominent in the Israeli-Palestinian conflict, where Israel's existence is perceived as a threat to Palestinians. Morrison's adoption of the IHRA definition of antisemitism, which emphasizes context, attempts to address this paradigm by acknowledging that antisemitism isn't solely tied to Israeli actions. However, his criticism of the UN for bias against Israel indicates he may still view the conflict as a zero-sum game, where gains for one side mean losses for the other.

Peter Dutton.

Opposition Leader Peter Dutton's stance on antisemitism in Australia mirrors that of Scott Morrison, exhibiting a staunch opposition to antisemitism, a fervent advocacy for Jewish rights, and unwavering support for Israel's policies. In the wake of the October 7 Hamas attack, Dutton unequivocally condemned the violence as a calculated assault on civilians and affirmed Israel's inherent right to self-defense. This position was consistent with the Executive Council of Australian Jewry (ECAJ), which labeled the attacks as war crimes and called upon Israel to undertake necessary defensive measures.

Dutton's criticism extended to Prime Minister Anthony Albanese, reproaching him for a perceived delayed response and concerns over de-escalation. He similarly criticized Foreign Affairs Minister Penny Wong for urging Israel to exercise 'restraint' amidst the militia attack. Dutton's outright rejection of calls for de-escalation, arguing they favor terrorists, underlines his robust support for Australia's Jewish community and his alignment with ECAJ's stance (Ransley, 2023).

Dutton also swiftly denounced the pro-Palestinian rally in Sydney's Lakemba that followed the October 7 attack, condemning the antisemitic slogans, which ranged from expressions of hate to calls for annihilation. He characterized the comments as antisemitic, unacceptable, and appalling, sentiments echoed by ECAJ co-CEO Alex Ryvchin, who described the rally as 'sickening,' stating, "It is no exaggeration to say that this has been one of the darkest days in the history of Jewish people."

In contrast, the Australian National Imams Council urged a balanced approach, advocating for consideration of the Palestinian perspective, with local Imam Ibrahim Dadoun portraying the attacks on Israel as acts of resistance and advocating Jihad as the only response to occupation, reflecting the multifaceted and contentious nature of the conflict (Coote, 2023).

Dutton's strong condemnation of antisemitic rhetoric at the rally underscores the need for a multifaceted approach to combat antisemitism, involving government, policymakers, and security agencies. Australia must foster a culture of zero tolerance towards jihadist rhetoric and ensure comprehensive education on historical atrocities to effectively eradicate antisemitism.

Dutton's critique of Prime Minister Albanese's handling of antisemitism underscores broader concerns about leadership and the necessity for a unified response to combat this pervasive hatred.

Furthermore, Dutton criticized the Albanese Government for what he perceived as a bias against Israel, accusing them of lacking moral clarity in distinguishing between lawful and unlawful actions, civilization and barbarism, good and evil. He advocated for a stringent approach to violence, promising that a future Coalition government would cancel visas and deport non-citizens who incite or engage in violence. In response, Prime Minister Albanese accused Dutton of politicizing antisemitism and emphasized the importance of fostering social cohesion amid the Israel-Gaza conflict.

Albanese condemned the politicization of antisemitism while reiterating his commitment to standing against it, supporting the rights and justice of the Palestinian people, and advocating for a two-state solution, all while emphasizing the need for community unity. This exchange occurred against a backdrop of pro-Palestinian protests targeting federal electoral offices, featuring bloodied replicas of Gazan corpses.

In June 2024, Dutton participated in the 'Behind the Scenes Conversation' event at Moriah College, where he received a standing ovation for his commitment to combating antisemitism and supporting Israel. Organized by Sharri Markson and Carole Pillemer, the event aimed to support the Jewish Community Appeal (JCA) and featured notable figures such as Senators Dave Sharma, Sarah Henderson, and Holly Hughes.

Dutton emphasized the need for unwavering support and clear policies to combat antisemitism, echoing Markson's concerns about the ongoing threat and criticizing the inaction of police and political leaders.

During his speech, Dutton expressed concerns about the potential risks posed by 'inadequately vetted Gazan refugees' admitted to Australia and called on the Labor party to address 'hard left and antisemitic factions.' He criticized university vice-chancellors for their handling of antisemitism on campuses and the police for their lack of law enforcement, asserting that he would adopt a zero-tolerance approach to such behavior.

His remarks were met with significant approval, underscoring his influence and support among segments of the Australian population concerned with antisemitism.

Dutton's condemnation of the October 7 attack and his defense of Israel's actions reflect broader sociological and historical patterns of antisemitic rhetoric and violence. Sociological studies have long highlighted the role of prejudice, stereotypes, and 'othering' processes in fueling hatred and violence against Jewish communities.

The endurance of antisemitism, from medieval blood libels to modern terrorism, underscores the necessity for robust leadership and a clear moral stance against such hatred. Psychological research corroborates how cognitive biases and in-group favoritism contribute to antisemitic attitudes and behaviors.

As the Australian Government continues to grapple with the surge in antisemitic incidents and violence, the Jewish community often finds itself in a precarious position. On January 4th, Peter Dutton emphasized the urgency of serious action against antisemitism, stating that Jewish community leaders should not have to plead for legal enforcement when their community is under threat.

He called for the government to fortify laws and reimburse the Jewish community for legal actions against such attacks, stressing that hate speech has no place in society.

Dutton voiced concerns about the current educational approach, advocating for a comprehensive understanding of the Holocaust and antisemitism in schools and universities, asserting that 'nothing short of a societal-wide effort is required to reject the forces of indoctrination and to bring about a renaissance of education' (Middleton, 2024).

In summary, Peter Dutton's unwavering commitment to combating antisemitic violence and promoting the safety and security of the Jewish community in Australia is evident in his resolute stance against antisemitism, his unequivocal condemnation of the October 7 Hamas attack, and his defense of Israel's right to self-defense.

Dutton's crusade against antisemitism highlights his dedication to addressing this issue at both national and international levels, emphasizing the need for strong leadership and clear policies. This position aligns with academic understandings of the historical, sociological, and psychological underpinnings of antisemitism, underscoring the importance of robust measures to counter this persistent threat.

Furthermore, Scott Morrison's unwavering stance against antisemitism has had a significant impact on Australia's foreign policy, demonstrating a clear commitment to combating antisemitism and supporting Israel in international forums. Morrison's efforts stand out in the complex context of the Israel-Palestine conflict, serving as a strong defense of Jewish rights.

Alongside Julia Gillard, Morrison has highlighted the severity and rise of antisemitism in Australia, emphasizing the urgent need for policymakers, government officials, academics, and stakeholders to act. A comprehensive understanding of Morrison's stance on antisemitism and Australia's position in the region requires analysis within the broader context of Australian foreign policy.

In conclusion, the need for decisive leadership and robust legislative action to create an inclusive and secure environment for all Australians is underscored by the Jewish community's frustration with the lack of national leadership in addressing antisemitism. This frustration is rooted in the belief that Holocaust survivors in Australia no longer feel safe, emphasizing the importance of a societal-wide effort to combat indoctrination and promote education on the Holocaust and antisemitism.

By fostering a culture of zero tolerance towards hate speech and ensuring comprehensive education on historical atrocities, Australia can strive towards a future where antisemitism is unequivocally condemned and eradicated.

Chapter Three Conclusion.

Antisemitism remains in a state of limbo, caught between efforts to combat genuine hatred and prejudice against Jews and the risk of infringing on free expression, political critique, and academic freedom. The divergent views of scholars, activists, and lawmakers highlight the ongoing struggle to balance the fight against antisemitism with the preservation of fundamental rights.

Achieving this balance requires careful consideration and nuanced approaches, as the discourse on antisemitism and the IHRA definition continues to evolve, shaping policies and debates. This underscores the need for ongoing dialogue and critical examination to ensure that efforts to combat antisemitism do not inadvertently undermine other essential freedoms.

The complexity of antisemitism is further compounded by political accusations and academic controversies. The importance of the Australian Jewish community in this fight cannot be overstated, as they have been vocal advocates for the IHRA definition and have played a crucial role in promoting its adoption by various councils, states, and political organizations. Their continued involvement and advocacy are essential in ensuring the effective implementation of the IHRA definition and the comprehensive combatting of antisemitism.

The role of Jewish organizations, such as the Anti-Defamation Commission led by Dr. Dvir Abramovich, in defining antisemitism underscores the necessity of allowing Jewish people, as the primary victims of antisemitism, to define it. This ensures that the definition is not shaped by judeophobes, thus preserving the integrity of efforts to combat antisemitism.

In this political maneuvering, the fate of antisemitism in Australia hangs in the balance as leaders and officials struggle to address the issue without politicizing it. The current Australian Government, led by Prime Minister Anthony Albanese, has faced criticism for its inadequate response to the surge in antisemitic incidents since the October 7 attack. Deputy Prime Minister Richard Marles has described the current level of antisemitism in Australia as the worst he has seen, yet the government's response has been insufficient, highlighting the power of political expediency over moral principle.

It is imperative that universities, political leaders, and policymakers prioritize the protection of Jewish students and citizens over politicking. They must cease to juggle the complex issues surrounding definitions of antisemitism and instead take decisive action against hate speech to safeguard democracy, social cohesion, and communal safety and security in Australia.

Chapter Four

Brothers in Arms:

The Jewish Solidarity in Combating Antisemitism

Introduction.

The Jewish community's response to antisemitism is marked by a strategic and unified approach that encompasses international campaigns, legal advocacy, and grassroots engagement. The World Jewish Congress's (WJC) **'No to Antisemitism'** campaign and the Anti-Defamation League's (ADL) **'Combatting Antisemitism'** program exemplify the efforts to raise awareness and educate the public about the dangers of antisemitism. These initiatives highlight the historical and contemporary manifestations of antisemitism, promoting tolerance and understanding globally.

Collaborative efforts, such as the WJC's partnership with the United Nations for 'International Holocaust Remembrance Day' and the ADL's alliances with other minority groups, underscore the importance of solidarity in combating hate speech and violence. Despite significant challenges, including political opposition and the rise of online hate speech, these international campaigns demonstrate the power of unified action and strategic collaboration in addressing antisemitic rhetoric and violence.

The Executive Council of Australian Jewry (ECAJ) exemplifies a multifaceted approach to combating antisemitism within Australia. The ECAJ's efforts include proactive documentation, legal advocacy, and international collaboration, all aimed at defending Jewish rights and promoting democratic principles. Leaders like Peter

Wertheim and Julie Nathan have faced significant personal risks in their relentless fight against antisemitism, emphasizing the urgency and seriousness of the issue.

The ECAJ's work highlights the necessity for Jewish organizations to unite against the rising tide of antisemitism, setting aside political differences to focus on common goals. Their advocacy for enhanced security measures, legal reforms, and educational initiatives underscores the critical role of a comprehensive and integrated approach in safeguarding Jewish communities and promoting social justice.

Jewish political leaders in Australia play a crucial role in addressing antisemitism through legislative initiatives and community support. Figures like Josh Frydenberg, Michael Danby, Mark Dreyfus, and Julian Leeser have significantly contributed to the fight against antisemitism, advocating for stringent measures to curb hate speech and protect Jewish Australians from discrimination and violence. Their leadership underscores the importance of political representation in ensuring the safety and well-being of the Jewish community.

The responses of these politicians highlight the need for continuous vigilance, education, and robust legal measures to counter antisemitism effectively. Their advocacy for enhanced security and comprehensive educational programs is vital in fostering a society that values and protects its diverse communities.

The recent surge in antisemitism underscores the necessity for ongoing and robust measures to combat this persistent threat. Jewish solidarity and strategic collaboration are essential in addressing the spectrum of antisemitic actions, from hate speech and boycotts to calls for annihilation. The collective response of Jewish academics, artists, and community leaders illustrates the power of unified action in fostering empathy and humanity.

Leaders like Jeremy Leibler and organizations such as the Australasian Union of Jewish Students emphasize the importance of grassroots engagement and integration within broader society. This strategic shift, combined with a proactive legal and policy framework, is crucial in building a resilient, empathetic, and inclusive society. Through solidarity and decisive action, the Jewish community can uphold the values of tolerance and mutual respect, ensuring a safer and more secure future for all.

4.1 United Against Hate: International Responses to Antisemitism.

The international fight against antisemitism has become increasingly urgent, with studies and opinion polls consistently highlighting a troubling rise in antisemitic rhetoric and violence. United Nations Secretary-General Antonio Guterres has noted that antisemitism "is on the rise in all parts of the world." This alarming trend underscores the broader threat that such hatred poses to modern democracies, the rule of law, and the protection of human rights.

During the COVID-19 pandemic, ancient antisemitic libels resurfaced, intertwined with conspiracy myths and religious intolerance, making Jews worldwide increasingly fearful of expressing their identity or practicing their religion freely. Effectively addressing antisemitism requires a comprehensive, multi-pronged approach involving the United Nations and parliaments worldwide. By enhancing efforts to combat antisemitism as a cross-cutting human rights issue, countries can help protect democratic values, peace, and societal stability.

In response to the surge in antisemitism, the international Jewish community has mobilized through key organizations such as the World Jewish Congress (WJC) and the Anti-Defamation League (ADL). These organizations have been instrumental in advocating for Jewish rights and combating antisemitism globally.

The WJC has been at the forefront, condemning antisemitic attacks and urging governments to protect Jewish communities. Engaging with international bodies like the United Nations, the WJC has raised awareness about the growing threat of antisemitism and pushed for stronger measures to counter it. This multifaceted approach demonstrates the Jewish community's commitment to combating hatred and ensuring the safety and dignity of Jews worldwide.

A notable example of the international Jewish response to antisemitism is the action taken by the WJC's NextGen members. In an unprecedented show of unity, over 80 NextGen members from more than 25 countries and over 55 campuses signed an open letter urging university administrators to protect Jewish students amidst rising antisemitism and anti-Israel activity on campuses.

This initiative followed the replication of a hostile encampment originally staged at Columbia University across numerous campuses, where Jewish students faced vile antisemitic slurs and harassment. The NextGen members' letter, sent to over 100 university presidents, calls for urgent measures to protect students and curb hate-driven activities. This collective effort underscores the critical role educational institutions play in combating antisemitism and fostering an atmosphere of safety and inclusivity.

In response to rising antisemitism in Europe, a delegation from the WJC recently visited Slovenia to engage with local and international stakeholders. Comprising Jews from eleven different countries, the delegation aimed to support Slovenia's small Jewish community, primarily based in Ljubljana. The visit involved high-level meetings with Slovenian government officials, the diplomatic community, and the International Holocaust Remembrance Alliance (IHRA) delegation.

These efforts focused on raising awareness about the challenges faced by the Jewish community, advocating for their right to live freely and safely, and garnering tangible support from both local and international authorities. The delegation's experience highlighted the power of high-level diplomacy and the importance of standing firm against prejudice, reaffirming the WJC's commitment to defending Jewish rights and ensuring the security and dignity of even the smallest Jewish communities.

In France, on October 24, the Special Envoys and Coordinators Combating Antisemitism (SECCA) meeting convened in Paris, under the auspices of the WJC, the European Commission, and UNESCO. UNESCO Director-General Audrey Azoulay emphasized the gravity of the meeting amid a global resurgence of antisemitism.

Katharina von Schnurbein of the European Commission expressed gratitude to the national envoys and Jewish community representatives for their dedication. France was represented by Mathias Dreyfuss and Delphine Borione, who contributed to discussions on the intersection of online hate and artificial intelligence, with META France also participating. The day concluded with a cultural event celebrating Sephardic Jewish heritage, underscoring the rich cultural contributions of the Jewish community.

Marie-Sarah Seeberger opened the discussions by reflecting on the multifaceted challenges faced by French Jews, including chants calling for Israel's disappearance and warnings to avoid certain Paris districts due to protests. She reported over 500 antisemitic incidents in France within just two weeks, illustrating the alarming rise in hostility. Seeberger highlighted the collaborative efforts between CRIF, French Jewish institutions, and the Ministry of Interior to ensure the safety of the Jewish community.

Emphasizing the imperative of solidarity and understanding, particularly for Jewish students facing daily challenges on campuses worldwide, the SECCA meeting underscored the critical need to address antisemitism comprehensively. The discussions aimed to combat isolation and ensure a safer environment for Jews in France and globally, advocating for policies and actions that protect and empower Jewish individuals and communities.

In the UK, the Jewish community has faced a significant rise in antisemitic incidents following the October 7 attack on Israel. The Community Security Trust (CST), a Jewish advisory body, reported a record 4,103 antisemitic incidents in 2023, the highest number since the organization began recording such data.

This surge represents a 400% increase since October 7, with over two-thirds of the incidents occurring on or after that date, averaging 31 incidents per day. These incidents encompass assaults, property damage, threats, verbal abuse, and online harassment. The CST has described this period as a 'watershed' moment, indicating a dramatic shift in the level of antisemitic hostility in the UK.

In response, the UK government has allocated £3 million in funding for the CST to enhance security at Jewish institutions. The Metropolitan Police have also pledged stronger action against hate crimes related to the Israel-Hamas conflict, resulting in over 400 arrests. Additionally, the government announced £7 million in increased funding over the next three years to address antisemitism in educational institutions.

The Jewish community has condemned the rise in antisemitic incidents, urging greater action to combat the issue. The CST has called for widespread condemnation of antisemitism, emphasizing the harassment, intimidation, threats, and attacks faced by British Jews in various settings, including schools, universities, workplaces, streets, and online.

Furthermore, at the Jerusalem Post Conference in June 2024, WJC President Ronald S. Lauder delivered a powerful address, expressing gratitude to the paper's dedication in keeping the audience informed. Speaking as an individual Jew, Lauder emphasized the importance of unity in facing challenges. He reflected on the aftermath of the October 7 attack on Israel, noting the initial global sympathy followed by a swift turn against Israel, orchestrated through a premeditated social media campaign.

Lauder underscored the significance of social media in shaping young people's views and highlighted the need for Israel to dominate social media to counter false narratives. He also addressed internal divisions within the Jewish community, urging unity in the face of external threats. Lauder's call to action emphasized the importance of individual and collective efforts in combating antisemitism and preserving Jewish identity.

In a similar vein, the Anti-Defamation League (ADL) has been at the forefront of the crusade against antisemitic rhetoric, playing a pivotal role in monitoring and documenting incidents of antisemitism globally. Through its rigorous analysis and advocacy, the ADL collaborates with governments, law enforcement agencies, and other stakeholders to devise effective strategies for preventing and responding to antisemitic attacks. A notable aspect of the ADL's efforts includes its criticism of Students for Justice in Palestine (SJP), a network of pro-Palestinian student groups in the United States.

The ADL accuses SJP of disseminating anti-Israel propaganda and employing aggressive tactics, such as disrupting pro-Israel events and constructing mock 'apartheid walls.' These chapters have been linked to violence, intimidation, and harassment against Jewish and pro-Israel students on campuses. Consequently, the ADL has called on universities to closely monitor SJP chapters and take disciplinary action when conduct codes are breached or other students are harassed.

In the wake of the Israel-Hamas conflict, the ADL has documented a significant uptick in antisemitic incidents, particularly in the Chicago area. The ADL's Midwest chapter released a report identifying several local pro-Palestinian groups, including the U.S. Palestinian Community Network, American Muslims for Palestine, and Jewish Voices for Peace, as contributors to the rise in antisemitic acts through activities such as protests and antisemitic social media posts. David Goldenberg, the director of the ADL's Midwest chapter, highlighted that the level of antisemitism in Chicago during the conflict surpassed previous years, necessitating urgent action against the spread of antisemitism on social media and other platforms.

The ADL's commitment to combating campus antisemitism is evident in its comprehensive assessment of 85 American universities. This assessment, part of the ADL's Campus Antisemitism Report Card, assigned grades based on universities' effectiveness in protecting Jewish students from hate. Institutions like Harvard received failing grades due to incidents of antisemitic vandalism, cartoons, and the blame placed on Israel by student coalitions for attacks.

The ADL's report also highlighted the need for universities to implement mandatory training and publicly condemn antisemitism, urging institutions like the University of Massachusetts-Amherst to address the hostile environment against Jewish students.

In a significant meeting in May 2024, Interim University President Alan M. Garber of Harvard engaged with ADL CEO Jonathan Greenblatt to tackle campus antisemitism. This meeting, set against the backdrop of congressional investigations and ongoing pro-Palestine encampments in Harvard Yard, underscored Harvard's commitment to addressing these issues. Greenblatt's praise for Garber's firm stance against negotiating with encampment protesters who demanded divestment from Israeli-affiliated entities exemplified the ADL's influence and its advocacy for stringent measures to protect Jewish students.

The ADL's Campus Antisemitism Report Card, an unprecedented initiative, provided a nuanced evaluation of university responses to antisemitism. Institutions such as Brandeis University and Elon University received top grades, while notable schools like MIT, Harvard, and Princeton were among those that failed. Jonathan Greenblatt emphasized the importance of creating safe and supportive campus environments, free from antisemitism, especially given its alarming prevalence. The report's development involved consultations with experts, including Jewish clergy and university leaders, reflecting a broad consensus on the need for robust measures against campus antisemitism.

Moreover, the ADL's continued vigilance is evident in its revised grades issued in June 2024, considering recent anti-Israel activities on campuses. The updated evaluations, part of the ADL's Not on My Campus campaign, highlighted the surge in hostility toward Jewish students and stressed the need for university leaders to prioritize student safety. The ADL's commitment to re-assessing grades based on new information underscores its dynamic approach to combating antisemitism, reinforcing the importance of a zero-tolerance policy on college campuses.

In summary, the international Jewish community has launched several significant initiatives and campaigns to raise awareness and combat antisemitism. The 'No to Antisemitism' campaign, initiated by the World Jewish Congress (WJC) in 2023, exemplifies these efforts. This campaign promotes tolerance and understanding by highlighting both the historical and contemporary manifestations of antisemitism and its profound impact on Jewish communities worldwide. By drawing attention to these issues, the campaign aims to foster a more informed and empathetic global society.

Another notable initiative is the 'Combatting Antisemitism' program, launched by the Anti-Defamation League (ADL) in 2022. This program focuses on educating the public about the dangers of antisemitism, promoting interfaith dialogue, and advocating for policy changes to counter hate speech and violence. The ADL has also formed strategic partnerships with organizations such as the Simon Wiesenthal Center to amplify its efforts and broaden its reach. These collaborations enhance the effectiveness of their campaigns by pooling resources and expertise.

Collaborative efforts and partnerships have been pivotal in addressing antisemitic rhetoric and violence. For instance, the WJC's partnership with the United Nations to promote

'International Holocaust Remembrance Day' underscores the importance of global cooperation in combating antisemitism. Joint statements and conferences held under this partnership aim to foster international solidarity and action against hate. Similarly, the ADL's collaboration with other minority groups, such as the African American and Latino communities, highlights the intersectionality of hate speech and violence, promoting a united front against all forms of discrimination.

In conclusion, despite these concerted efforts, the international Jewish community continues to face significant challenges in combating antisemitism. Political opposition remains a major hurdle, with some governments and political leaders accused of downplaying or outright denying the existence of antisemitism.

This lack of acknowledgment hampers efforts to address and mitigate antisemitic incidents effectively. Additionally, the rise of hate speech online presents a formidable challenge, as digital platforms have become breeding grounds for antisemitic rhetoric and incitement to violence.

Global geopolitical tensions further exacerbate these challenges. The ongoing conflict between Israel and Hamas, for instance, has heightened tensions and violence, providing fertile ground for antisemitic groups and individuals to propagate hate speech and incite violence against Jewish communities. These dynamics underscore the need for sustained and multifaceted approaches to combat antisemitism, involving education, policy advocacy, and international collaboration.

While significant progress has been made through various campaigns and initiatives, the fight against antisemitism is far from over. Continuous efforts, strategic partnerships, and unwavering commitment are essential to overcoming the persistent and evolving challenges posed by antisemitism worldwide.

4.2 Guardians of Identity: The ECAJ's Campaign against Antisemitic Rhetoric.

In Australia, the Executive Council of Australian Jewry (ECAJ) serves as the primary representative body for the Jewish community, leading efforts to combat antisemitism. Recognizing the historical and persistent nature of this issue, the ECAJ has taken a proactive approach in addressing antisemitic incidents across the country.

Through its annual reports, the ECAJ meticulously documents the rise in antisemitic acts, including physical assaults, graffiti, and online hate speech. In response, the council has advocated for enhanced governmental support and funding for security measures within Jewish communities, alongside improved educational programs and media representations to counter antisemitic narratives.

Internationally, the ECAJ represents the Australian Jewish community at forums like the World Jewish Congress, fostering dialogue with diverse ethnic and religious groups within Australia. The council actively engages in human rights discussions with the Australian government, providing valuable insights on issues pertinent to the Jewish community. Furthermore, the ECAJ plays a pivotal role in supporting various Jewish institutions, including educational, healthcare, welfare services, and religious establishments. Its commitment to advancing democratic principles, human rights, and social justice underscores the ECAJ's broader mission of promoting these values within both the Australian Jewish community and society at large.

As the ECAJ addresses the international context of antisemitism, particularly concerning Israel, it has been vocal about decisions made by international bodies such as the International Court of Justice (ICJ) that impact the region. The council released a statement criticizing the ICJ's ruling on the Israeli-Palestinian conflict, describing it as a 'death sentence' for Israeli hostages held in Gaza and a blow to international law and peace. The ECAJ emphasized that Israel has taken unprecedented precautions to avoid civilian harm in conflict, underscoring the necessity of dismantling the capabilities of groups like Hamas to ensure regional stability.

This stance aligns with President Daniel Aghion's emphasis on taking legal action against individuals and organizations propagating antisemitism. His condemnation of hateful Jihadi rhetoric and call for broader societal condemnation underscore the ECAJ's commitment to defending the Jewish community's honor and ensuring Australia's future as a peaceful society.

Aghion has particularly stressed the urgent need to address hate speech from extremist Islamic preachers and has criticized the lack of adequate response from other leaders. As Aghion stated, "The hate preaching must stop now. There are multiple ethnic and faith communities in Australia, and the last thing we need is for our peaceful and cohesive society to be ruined by the importation into Australia of the hatreds and violence of overseas conflicts." This highlights the ECAJ's determination to combat antisemitism and promote social harmony across diverse communities

Under Aghion's leadership, the ECAJ has also taken a firm stance against antisemitism and privacy violations, particularly in response to the recent doxing of Jewish individuals. Aghion condemned the publication of lists containing personal information of hundreds of Jewish individuals, highlighting the resulting harassment, death threats, professional and financial loss, vandalism, and psychological harm inflicted upon them. He likened these actions to practices of the Nazi era and called for legal reform to make doxing illegal, emphasizing that such practices have no place in a free and democratic society.

The ECAJ's response to these issues includes urging social media platforms to permanently deactivate accounts used for doxing and providing support for individuals affected by these attacks. Aghion expressed gratitude for the support from members of parliament and affirmed the ECAJ's commitment to working with them to protect victims and hold perpetrators accountable.

Prime Minister Anthony Albanese has responded to these concerns, promising legislation to address doxing. The ECAJ's response underscores its dedication to combating antisemitism and ensuring the safety and well-being of the Jewish community in Australia.

Robert Goot, Deputy President of the ECAJ and affiliated with the World Jewish Congress, has been tasked with establishing a WJC task force on responses to antisemitism. The aim of the task force is to examine, monitor, assess, recommend, assist, and coordinate responses to antisemitism among the affiliated communities, organizations, and regions of the WJC. This initiative comes in response to a significant increase in antisemitic incidents globally since October 7, highlighting the urgent need for coordinated action against antisemitism.

Furthermore, Peter Wertheim, Co-CEO of the ECAJ, has played a significant role in advocating against antisemitism in Australia. He has highlighted the need for increased government support and funding for security measures within the Jewish community. Additionally, Wertheim has emphasized the importance of education and media representation in countering antisemitic narratives.

His efforts aim to promote human rights and ensure the safety of the Australian Jewish community. Wertheim has also criticized the lack of legal action against hate speech and threats of violence targeting Jews, calling for tougher legislation to deter such behavior.

At a Senate inquiry into right-wing radicalism, Wertheim pointed out the alarming convergence of extremist groups in their antisemitic rhetoric. He noted that neo-Nazis and pro-Islam groups often share similar messages, blurring the lines between left- and right-wing extremism. This convergence poses a significant threat that requires urgent attention.

Wertheim's concerns were echoed by Colin Rubenstein, Executive Director of the Australia/Israel and Jewish Affairs Council, who criticized the inquiry's narrow scope and emphasized the need to consider various forms of extremism to understand the challenges faced by Jewish Australians. Rubenstein supported the 'horseshoe theory,' suggesting that extremist groups from different ends of the political spectrum converge in their hostility towards Jewish people.

The ECAJ has also expressed deep concern over the rise of antisemitism on university campuses. Peter Wertheim and Alex Ryvchin have both highlighted the need for a judicial inquiry into the surge of antisemitic incidents on Australian campuses. Wertheim stated that a judicial inquiry is necessary to investigate the adequacy of university administrations' responses to antisemitism, arguing that only such an inquiry can provide the necessary focus and impartiality. This call for action underscores the ECAJ's commitment to ensuring that universities remain places of respectful exchange and safe engagement for all students and academics.

Alex Ryvchin, ECAJ Executive Officer, has been particularly vocal about the disturbing trends of antisemitism on university campuses. He emphasizes that the rise of anti-Jewish sentiment is not merely a matter of isolated incidents but reflects a broader and more systemic issue within academic institutions.

Ryvchin has noted that antisemitic rhetoric and actions have created hostile environments for Jewish students, threatening their right to education and safety. He argues, "Universities should be sanctuaries of learning and free exchange of ideas, yet they are increasingly becoming hotbeds of hate and intolerance."

Ryvchin's concerns are backed by reports of Jewish students facing harassment, exclusion, and intimidation on campus. He has highlighted specific instances where Jewish students have been singled out and ostracized during campus events, noting that these experiences have profound psychological impacts on those affected. "Jewish students are being targeted and marginalized, simply for their identity and their support for Israel," Ryvchin stated, underscoring the urgent need for comprehensive measures to address these issues.

Ryvchin has pointed out that many universities have failed to take adequate measures to protect Jewish students, often downplaying or ignoring reports of antisemitism. He contends, "The lack of decisive action by university authorities is tantamount to tacit approval of antisemitic behavior. This is unacceptable and must be addressed through a judicial inquiry."

The ECAJ's advocacy for a judicial inquiry reflects its broader mission to combat antisemitism in all its forms and ensure the safety and dignity of Jewish individuals. By calling for this inquiry, Ryvchin and Wertheim are not only seeking justice for the victims of campus antisemitism but also aiming to set a precedent for how such issues should be handled in the future. Ryvchin's insistence that "only a judicial inquiry can provide the necessary focus and impartiality" highlights the ECAJ's commitment to a thorough and fair investigation, ensuring that universities uphold their responsibilities to all students and maintain environments conducive to learning and mutual respect.

In conclusion, the ECAJ's multifaceted approach to combating antisemitism involves proactive documentation, advocacy for legal and social measures, and international collaboration. Its unwavering defense of Jewish rights and commitment to Israel underscores its broader mission of promoting democratic principles, human rights, and social justice.

Through its efforts, the ECAJ aims to foster a society where all individuals can live without fear of discrimination or violence, maintaining Australia's reputation as a peaceful and inclusive nation. As the Guardian of Identity, the ECAJ stands as a beacon against the tide of antisemitism, ensuring the preservation of Jewish heritage and the protection of Jewish communities in Australia and beyond.

In the face of criticism and challenges, the Executive Council of Australian Jewry (ECAJ) has remained steadfast in its mission to advocate for Jewish rights and combat antisemitism in Australia. Despite accusations of narrow representation and political alignment, the ECAJ has continued its vital work, often at personal risk to its leaders like Peter Wertheim and Julie Nathan, who have faced threats and slurs from extremists. These incidents underscore the urgency and seriousness of the battle against antisemitism, which affects not only the safety of individuals but also the broader Jewish community's livelihood. Thus, the ECAJ exemplifies resilience and determination, leading the charge against hate and bigotry to ensure a brighter, more inclusive future for all.

Moreover, it is crucial for Jewish organizations to set aside politicking and hair-splitting over definitions and rhetoric and unite against the rising tide of antisemitism in Australia. As Israel faces an existential war, its impacts are felt across the global Jewish community. The ECAJ's unwavering commitment to this cause serves as a beacon, highlighting the necessity for unity and decisive action. By focusing on common goals and standing together, Jewish organizations can present a stronger front against antisemitism, ensuring a safer and more secure future for all Jewish people, both in Australia and around the world.

4.3 Beyond the Call of Duty: Jewish Politicians' Response to Antisemitism.

The responses of Jewish politicians in Australia to the rise of antisemitism highlight the crucial role of political leadership in combating this pervasive issue. Figures such as Josh Frydenberg, Michael Danby, Mark Dreyfus, and Julian Leeser serve as exemplary cases among many other dedicated leaders who have tirelessly advocated for the Jewish community's protection and rights.

Their efforts, encompassing advocacy, legislative initiatives, and community support, illustrate the multifaceted approach required to address antisemitism effectively. These politicians exemplify the broader commitment of Jewish political leaders to ensuring the safety and well-being of Jewish Australians.

The contributions of these politicians underscore the necessity for a unified governmental and community response to antisemitism. Through their advocacy, they highlight the importance of continued vigilance, comprehensive education, and robust legal measures to combat discrimination and hate.

As antisemitism continues to pose a significant challenge, the leadership and advocacy of Jewish politicians remain essential in fostering a secure and inclusive environment for the Jewish community in Australia.

Josh Frydenberg.

Josh Frydenberg, a leading Jewish politician, has been a prominent figure in the fight against antisemitism in Australia. As a senior member of the Australian government, Frydenberg has consistently condemned antisemitic incidents, emphasizing the necessity of a unified governmental and community response. In 2023, he denounced the surge of antisemitic attacks on university campuses, calling them "completely unacceptable" and vowing that the government would ensure the safety and well-being of Jewish students.

Frydenberg's efforts extend beyond condemnation; he has been active in providing funding for security measures and educational programs aimed at combating antisemitism. His support for Holocaust education, particularly following severe cases of antisemitic bullying in Melbourne schools, underscores his commitment to addressing the root causes of hatred.

Frydenberg's proactive stance is further highlighted by his hosting of the documentary 'Never Again: The Fight Against Antisemitism,' where he underscored the importance of turning the words 'never again' into concrete actions. This documentary reflects his dedication to educating the public and fostering a deeper understanding of the dangers of antisemitism.

Frydenberg's advocacy is multifaceted, combining immediate protective measures with long-term educational strategies to combat hatred and ensure the safety of the Jewish community. His comprehensive approach to addressing antisemitism has garnered widespread praise and recognition, both within Australia and internationally, affirming his leadership role in the fight against this persistent issue.

Michael Danby.

Michael Danby, a former member of the Australian Parliament, has made significant contributions to the fight against antisemitism through his legislative and advocacy efforts. Throughout his political career, Danby has been a vocal advocate for raising awareness about antisemitism and implementing robust measures to counter its rise. His unwavering support for Israel and condemnation of anti-Israel sentiments that veer into antisemitism are well-documented.

For instance, in 2018, Danby criticized the University of Sydney Student Representative Council for endorsing the Boycott, Divestment, and Sanctions (BDS) movement, describing it as a thinly veiled attempt to delegitimize Israel. This stance underscores his commitment to defending the Jewish state and combating efforts that threaten its legitimacy.

Danby has also been a strong proponent of stricter laws to combat hate speech and incitement, advocating for increased funding for security measures within the Jewish community. His proactive approach includes calling for more resources to protect Jewish institutions and individuals from potential threats.

In 2023, Danby's response to an international incident in the Polish parliament, where an MP discharged a fire extinguisher at a Hanukkah menorah, highlighted his commitment to combating antisemitism both domestically and internationally. He condemned the act as "appalling" and called for decisive action, reflecting his dedication to addressing antisemitism wherever it arises. Danby's multifaceted approach, combining legislative action with community support, demonstrates his comprehensive commitment to combating antisemitism and ensuring the safety and well-being of the Jewish community.

Mark Dreyfus.

Mark Dreyfus, a prominent Jewish politician and member of the Labor Party, has been an unwavering advocate in the fight against antisemitism. Serving as the Shadow Attorney-General, Dreyfus has consistently used his platform to condemn the surge in antisemitic incidents and rhetoric across the country. His advocacy reflects a deep commitment to addressing this persistent issue and ensuring that Jewish Australians are protected from discrimination and hate.

A notable example of Dreyfus' efforts was his response to the rise of antisemitism on Australian university campuses in 2023. Dreyfus criticized university administrations for their insufficient action, stating that their failure to address the issue was "tantamount to tacit approval of antisemitic behavior." He called for a judicial inquiry into the matter, arguing that only such an inquiry could provide the necessary focus and impartiality to thoroughly investigate the problem and the adequacy of the universities' responses.

This stance underscored the urgency of the situation and the need for decisive action to protect Jewish students and ensure that universities remain safe and inclusive environments.

In addition to his advocacy on university campuses, Dreyfus has been vocal about the broader rise of antisemitism in Australia. He has condemned the proliferation of hate speech and online harassment targeting the Jewish community and called for stronger legal measures to combat these forms of discrimination. Dreyfus emphasized the importance of education and community engagement in addressing the root causes of antisemitism, fostering dialogue and understanding between the Jewish community and other groups.

His commitment to combating antisemitism is further exemplified by his legislative efforts. On November 28, 2023, Dreyfus stated, "There is absolutely no place in Australia for hatred, violence, and anti-Semitism," and announced plans to introduce amendments making the Nazi salute a criminal offense under Commonwealth law. He reinforced this on November 30, 2023, saying, "There is no place in Australia for symbols that glorify the horrors of the Holocaust... Today, the Albanese Labor government is strengthening our legislation to ensure that never again will anyone in this country be allowed to celebrate or profit from acts and symbols of the Nazis and terrorist organizations."

These efforts underscore his role as a key ally and advocate for the Jewish community in Australia, committed to ensuring that the horrors of the past are never forgotten or repeated.

Julian Leeser.

Julian Leeser, another key figure in the fight against antisemitism, has been proactive in condemning antisemitic incidents and advocating for the protection of Jewish Australians. In 2023, Leeser vociferously condemned the rise of antisemitic attacks on university campuses, emphasizing the critical need for a unified governmental and community response to this growing threat.

He criticized the Australian Human Rights Commission (AHRC) for its perceived failure to adequately address antisemitism, accusing it of being "frozen by political paralysis." Leeser pointed out that while the commission focused on protecting pro-Palestine protesters, it neglected the alarming rise of antisemitism. He cited a 738% increase in antisemitic attacks reported by the Executive Council of Australian Jewry (ECAJ), highlighting the severity of the issue and the commission's inadequate response.

In response to the growing antisemitism, particularly on university campuses, Leeser introduced a bill aimed at curbing these incidents. He specifically criticized universities for their failure to recognize the specific nature of antisemitism and its contemporary manifestations. Leeser underscored the necessity for universities to address antisemitic behavior decisively and comprehensively.

Amid rising tensions over the Israel-Hamas conflict, Leeser vowed not to walk down a "path of silence and fear," instead advocating for robust measures to protect Jewish Australians. His call for action included enhancing security measures and fostering a zero-tolerance policy towards antisemitism in educational institutions, thereby ensuring that Jewish students can learn in a safe and inclusive environment.

In Summary, the responses of Jewish politicians in Australia to the rise of antisemitism demonstrate a profound commitment to combating this pernicious issue through advocacy, legislative initiatives, and community support. Josh Frydenberg, Michael Danby, Mark Dreyfus, and Julian Leeser have each contributed significantly to the fight against antisemitism, employing various strategies to address the problem comprehensively.

Their efforts underscore the importance of a unified response from both the government and the community, highlighting the need for continued vigilance, education, and robust legal measures to protect Jewish Australians from discrimination and hate. As antisemitism continues to pose a significant challenge, the leadership and advocacy of these politicians remain crucial in ensuring the safety and well-being of the Jewish community in Australia.

The necessity of Jewish political representation in Australia is paramount in ensuring the protection of Jewish rights, safeguarding their well-being, and advocating for stringent measures to curb the ongoing violent antisemitic rhetoric emanating from both white supremacists and Islamic radicals. Violent pro-Palestinian protests have significantly impacted Jewish communities, forcing many to relocate, close their businesses, and prevent Jewish students from attending schools and universities.

These disruptions not only threaten the physical safety of Jewish individuals but also undermine their economic stability and educational opportunities. The psychological impact of living in fear and the community's sense of vulnerability cannot be overstated.

In conclusion, Jewish political leaders play an essential role in addressing these multifaceted challenges. They advocate for enhanced security measures, ensure the enforcement of anti-hate speech laws, and work to foster a societal understanding of the unique manifestations of antisemitism. It is critical to implement comprehensive educational programs that highlight the dangers of antisemitism and promote tolerance and inclusion.

Additionally, political leaders must continue to push for judicial inquiries into the failings of institutions, such as universities, in addressing antisemitic incidents, ensuring accountability and reform.

The experiences of Jewish communities facing violent pro-Palestinian protests serve as a stark reminder of the ongoing struggle against antisemitism. The unwavering dedication of Jewish political leaders is vital in fostering an environment where Jewish Australians can live without fear, thrive economically, and pursue their educational aspirations without hindrance. Their leadership and advocacy are indispensable in creating a society that values and protects its diverse communities, ensuring that antisemitism is effectively confronted and eradicated.

4.4 Solidarity and Strategy: Jewish Community's Response to Antisemitism.

The Jewish community in Australia, numbering approximately 100,000 individuals, has exhibited a profound sense of abandonment and distress in response to escalating antisemitism, as highlighted in an open letter coordinated by Melbourne-based writer Lee Kofman. This letter, endorsed by a diverse cohort of Australian Jewish scholars, journalists, and creative professionals, underscores a collective unease and a perceived disconnect between the broader society's professed progressive ideals and the lived experiences of Jewish Australians.

Kofman's poignant remark, "It really shook us to the core of our identity. We belong to this progressive tribe, but the progressive tribe doesn't seem to have very progressive values when it comes to us Jews," captures a critical juncture in Australia's multicultural fabric. This statement reflects the Jewish community's struggle to reconcile its identity with a society that often falls short of its own standards of inclusivity and tolerance.

The open letter not only articulates the immediate repercussions of antisemitic incidents on the Jewish community's sense of security and belonging but also raises fundamental questions about Australia's commitment to fostering a truly inclusive, empathetic, and harmonious societal ethos, particularly during times of adversity and conflict. This sentiment mirrors a broader concern within the Jewish community regarding the erosion of trust and safety, as well as a perceived failure of the broader society to uphold its professed values of tolerance and inclusivity.

The letter's significance lies in its urgent call for a deeper understanding and empathy towards the experiences of Jewish Australians, particularly in light of the rise in antisemitic incidents. It stands as a testament to the resilience and determination of the Jewish community to confront and address the challenges posed by antisemitism while advocating for a more inclusive and empathetic society for all Australians.

In a collective response to the growing antisemitism, more than 520 Jewish academics and artists have united to call for empathy and humanity in the face of profound collective grief. This response underscores the gravity of antisemitism's impact on artists in Australia, as evidenced by the experiences of Jewish creatives who face ostracism, threats, and professional repercussions due to their support for Israel.

The doxing of 600 Jewish creatives in February, including prominent figures like Lee Kofman and Anita Lester, illustrates the extent of this hostility. The leaked private WhatsApp chat, intended as a support group for Australian Jewish artists post-October 7, led to public backlash and work cancellations, tarnishing the professional reputations of those involved. Kofman's description of the Australian arts community as "more antisemitic than I ever suspected" reflects the pervasive bias against Israel among many in the sector.

In the realm of academia, Alissa Foster, the president of the Australasian Union of Jewish Students (AUJS), has been vocal about the challenges faced by Jewish students on university campuses. Reflecting on a survey that revealed 64% of Australian Jewish university students experience antisemitism, Foster emphasizes the need for a cultural shift within universities. She calls for improved reporting systems, policy assessments, and accessible support for affected students. Despite the alarming figures, Foster notes that 85% of Jewish students do not report their experiences to the university, citing a lack of confidence in the university's ability to address the issue.

This reluctance to report highlights the deep-seated nature of the problem and the urgent need for action. Foster's discussions with MPs and senators in Canberra, alongside Jeremy Leibler, about the survey's results are crucial steps in raising awareness and advocating for change. Her hope is that the survey results will prompt meaningful action and encourage universities to adopt the IHRA definition of antisemitism, fostering a safer and more inclusive environment for all students.

In response to the surge in antisemitism following the October 7 attacks, Jeremy Leibler, President of the Zionist Federation of Australia, advocates for a proactive and outward-facing approach. Speaking at a B'nai B'rith meeting at Beth Weizmann, Leibler emphasized the need for a strategic shift, moving away from reliance on relationships with key decision-makers to investing in grassroots engagement.

He highlighted that "a very slow, sophisticated infiltration by anti-Israel groups into almost every single part of civil society, from the law to politics to education," necessitates a robust presence in these areas. This analysis underscores the necessity of a more comprehensive and integrated approach to combating antisemitism.

Leibler categorically rejected the notion that Australian political leaders, such as Prime Minister Anthony Albanese and Foreign Minister Penny Wong, are antisemitic, despite policy disagreements. He asserted, "We can have policy disagreements and critique rhetoric, but I can absolutely tell you emphatically that neither the Prime Minister nor the Foreign Minister are antisemites. It is completely counterproductive to throw that accusation around." This perspective reinforces his call for constructive engagement and dialogue rather than retreat and accusation, advocating for a more nuanced understanding of political dynamics.

Emphasizing the importance of outward engagement, Leibler articulated the need for the Jewish community to contribute to and benefit from broader Australian society. He stated, "We have something to contribute to this country, and we also have something to gain from being a part of broader society. I don't think we should allow our enemies to define us or how we operate in the real world."

This approach seeks to maintain a positive Jewish identity and effectively counter antisemitism by fostering integration and mutual benefit within the wider community. Leibler's strategy highlights the importance of resilience and proactive engagement in the face of growing antisemitism.

Additionally, Leibler shared his experience of visiting Israel shortly after the October 7 attacks, where he found solace in the solidarity among Israelis and the global Jewish community. "What we're all collectively feeling in Australia and across the Jewish world is what Jewish peoplehood feels like. If we can channel this pain into something meaningful and positive, we will do what Jews have done for generations: turn trauma into a pathway for rebuilding," he said.

Encouraging more Australian Jews to visit Israel, Leibler believes, will strengthen community bonds and foster resilience. He remains hopeful that the national unity in Israel, which transcended religious, political, and ethnic differences during recent conflicts, will continue to serve as a guideline for Jewish communities worldwide. Leibler's message is clear: the Jewish community must not let antisemitism define their identity or future.

In a manner akin to his son Jeremy, Mark Leibler AC, who serves as National Chair of the Australia Israel & Jewish Affairs Council (AIJAC), Life Chair of the Federal United Israel Appeal (UIA), and a Governor of the Australia-Israel Chamber of Commerce, has been an unwavering advocate against antisemitism.

Leibler asserts that "Zionism is about Jewishness. So, anti-Zionism is antisemitism," a statement that underscores his commitment to protecting Jewish identity and rights within Australia. He has called upon university leaders to defend Jewish students, questioning how, despite the Prime Minister acknowledging an antisemitism crisis on campuses, some university chancellors remain in denial.

Leibler's commentary highlights the urgent need for action as Australia faces a critical juncture, with protests and acts of defiance against orders to disband encampments on university grounds. He warns that these actions, coupled with the indifference of some academic leaders, could edge society closer to anarchy, where the rule of law is overshadowed by unchecked protester actions.

Drawing parallels with the situation at Harvard University, where similar issues have prompted serious dialogues, Leibler stresses the damaging impacts of discrimination and violence, urging politicians to address these challenges promptly before they escalate further. His call to action reflects a broader appeal for societal resilience and a reaffirmation of core values in combating antisemitism and ensuring a harmonious, inclusive environment for all.

Echoing Leibler's concerns, Jewish Labor MP Josh Burns has voiced deep concerns about the alarming rise in antisemitism in Australia, describing the situation as unprecedented. "I think the numbers reflect that there's been over a 700 percent increase in antisemitism in the last few months since October 7," he stated. Burns highlighted the need for unity in addressing this surge in hatred, emphasizing that the current moment requires collective action to combat antisemitism effectively. His call for solidarity comes amidst a backdrop of heightened tensions and violent incidents targeting Jewish individuals and institutions across the country.

The escalation of antisemitic acts has had a profound impact on Burns personally and professionally, particularly following an attack on his Melbourne office. Describing the incident as a "dangerous escalation," Burns expressed fears that such actions could lead to someone getting seriously hurt or worse. He noted that the incident had been condemned by Prime Minister Anthony Albanese, who called for the perpetrators to face the full force of the law. Burns also pointed out the broader implications of these attacks, underscoring how they undermine the values of inclusivity and respect that Australian society strives to uphold.

Reflecting on the broader implications of this rising antisemitism, Burns stressed the need for respectful communication and dialogue across different communities. He highlighted his long-standing relationships with Muslim ministers such as Ed Husic and Anne Aly, noting the importance of maintaining a space for respectful dialogue and disagreement. Burns reiterated his support for a two-state solution, expressing his hope for a future where a peace agreement between Israelis and Palestinians could bring an end to decades of conflict.

Despite the challenges, Burns remains committed to advocating for the rights and safety of the Jewish community in Australia, emphasizing the importance of unity and empathy in these turbulent times.

Similarly, Dr. Dvir Abramovich, Chairman of the Anti-Defamation Commission (ADC), has been a steadfast leader in the fight against antisemitism, leaving no nook and cranny untouched in Australia. He has strongly condemned acts of hatred and violence, such as the shocking anti-Semitic graffiti targeting Melbourne's Mount Scopus College, where the words "Jew die" were spray-painted on the front fence. Abramovich described this graffiti as "an assault on our safety," emphasizing the intensity and brutality of the message.

His personal connection to the school, as a former student, adds depth to his condemnation, highlighting the personal impact of such incidents on the Jewish community. Abramovich's statement reflects a deep concern for the safety and well-being of Jewish Australians and a determination to combat the spread of antisemitism.

Additionally, Abramovich has been instrumental in honoring individuals who stand against antisemitism and discrimination. He presented Indigenous Olympian Nova Peris with the ADC's Bravery Against Antisemitism Medal, recognizing her courageous stand against hate and her support for the Jewish community.

Abramovich praised Peris for her commitment to social change and her advocacy for respect and tolerance, highlighting her as a positive role model and a champion against bigotry. This recognition underscores Abramovich's efforts to highlight and commend those who actively combat antisemitism and promote inclusivity and understanding in society.

Despite these efforts, Abramovich has expressed grave concerns about the current state of antisemitism in Australia, describing it as "spiraling out of control." He has called for urgent action from the government to confront the "skyrocketing" antisemitism, particularly following the October 7 terror attacks and the Israel-Hamas war. Abramovich's statements highlight the urgency of the situation and the need for decisive measures to address the rise of antisemitism, emphasizing the importance of pushing back against hate and intolerance at all levels of society.

Commensurate with the ADC, the Australian Jewish Association (AJA) has condemned the recent rise in antisemitism in Australia, particularly in response to reports of antisemitic chants and threats. Pro-Palestinian protestors in Sydney reportedly chanted antisemitic expletives during a protest, and unverified reports suggest that Arabs in Melbourne are "**hunting for Jews**." The AJA has expressed concern over the potential disruption of Jewish vigils in Australia by these protestors, which could lead to increased hostilities between Palestinian and Israeli communities and sporadic violent confrontations.

Considering these events, the AJA has highlighted the increased likelihood of synagogues becoming targets for vandalism, leading to heightened security measures around Jewish holy sites. The organization has emphasized the need for police to investigate vandalism cases as hate crimes, especially amidst the ongoing Israeli-Hamas conflict.

Additionally, the AJA has raised concerns about the potential increase in antisemitic protests worldwide, where protestors may burn Israeli flags and blame Israeli policies in Palestine for ongoing conflicts, potentially legitimizing terrorist actions against Israel.

The AJA is closely monitoring the government's response to these protests, as it is likely to influence similar rallies worldwide. The organization expects governments to denounce reports of antisemitic chants and review the legality of such protests, which could determine the continuation, additional authorization, or cessation of future rallies.

The AJA's focus remains on safeguarding Australian Jewish communities, members of the Australian diplomatic mission in Israel, Jewish Australian nationals abroad, AJA members, Jewish tourists in Australia, and Israeli tourists in Australia from the impacts of rising antisemitism. By advocating for stronger governmental responses and legal frameworks, the AJA aims to ensure the protection and well-being of these vulnerable groups in the face of increasing hostility.

In conclusion, the recent surge in antisemitism highlights the necessity for ongoing and robust measures to combat this pernicious threat. The community's sense of abandonment, as articulated in an open letter by Lee Kofman, highlights the urgency of addressing antisemitism not only as isolated incidents but as part of a broader societal challenge.

To effectively counter the spectrum of antisemitic actions, from hate speech and boycotts to outright calls for annihilation, there must be a comprehensive legal framework and policy recommendations that fortify the protection of Jewish communities.

This requires a multi-faceted approach, encompassing improved reporting systems, rigorous investigation of hate crimes, and proactive educational campaigns that promote tolerance and inclusivity. The AJA's call for the government to denounce antisemitic chants and to scrutinize the legality of protests is a critical step towards ensuring that such hateful rhetoric is not normalized or ignored.

Moreover, Jewish solidarity and strategic collaboration are vital in this fight against antisemitism. The collective response of over 520 Jewish academics and artists calling for empathy and humanity illustrates the power of unified action. These examples, though significant, are merely a few among many that demonstrate the resilience and determination of the Jewish community. Leaders like Jeremy Leibler emphasize the need for grassroots engagement and integration within broader society to combat the sophisticated infiltration of anti-Israel sentiment into various civil sectors.

Similarly, the advocacy by Alissa Foster and the Australasian Union of Jewish Students highlights the necessity of fostering a safe and inclusive environment on university campuses. This strategic solidarity, combined with a proactive legal and policy framework, is essential to not only address the immediate threats but also to build a resilient, empathetic, and inclusive society that upholds the values of tolerance and mutual respect.

Chapter Four Conclusion.

The persistent and evolving nature of antisemitism necessitates robust measures and unwavering commitment from Jewish communities and their allies. The initiatives and responses detailed in this chapter underscore the multifaceted approach required to counter antisemitic rhetoric and violence effectively.

A critical component of this strategy is the implementation of comprehensive legal frameworks and policy recommendations. Strengthening hate crime reporting systems, conducting rigorous investigations, and enforcing anti-hate speech laws are essential steps to protect Jewish communities from discrimination and violence. Additionally, proactive educational campaigns that promote tolerance and inclusivity can help mitigate the spread of antisemitic ideologies.

Jewish solidarity plays a pivotal role in this fight against antisemitism. The collective efforts of organizations like the World Jewish Congress (WJC) and the Anti-Defamation League (ADL) illustrate the power of unified action. By fostering strategic collaborations with other minority groups and international bodies, these organizations amplify their impact and promote a united front against hate.

The importance of Jewish solidarity is further highlighted by the ECAJ's steadfast advocacy and the resilience of its leaders in the face of adversity.

Moreover, the responses of Jewish politicians and community leaders in Australia exemplify the critical role of political representation in combating antisemitism. Their advocacy for enhanced security measures, legal reforms, and educational initiatives underscores the necessity of a comprehensive and integrated approach.

The leadership of individuals like Josh Frydenberg, Michael Danby, Mark Dreyfus, and Julian Leeser demonstrates the importance of political engagement in safeguarding Jewish rights and promoting social justice.

In addressing antisemitism, it is essential to adopt a strategic shift that emphasizes grassroots engagement and constructive dialogue. By integrating into broader society and contributing to its development, the Jewish community can foster mutual respect and understanding. This approach not only counters antisemitism but also enhances the resilience and cohesion of the Jewish community.

Reflections on Jewish solidarity and the significance of turning trauma into a pathway for rebuilding highlight the community's resilience and proactive engagement. The advocacy of Alissa Foster and the Australasian Union of Jewish Students, for instance, underscores the importance of creating safe and inclusive environments on university campuses. By fostering empathy and humanity, the Jewish community can transform adversity into strength, ensuring a brighter and more inclusive future for all.

In conclusion, combating antisemitism requires a sustained and multifaceted approach that combines legal measures, educational initiatives, and strategic solidarity. The resilience and determination of the Jewish community, coupled with robust policy frameworks and international collaboration, are essential in addressing the challenges posed by antisemitism.

As '**Brothers in Arms**,' the Jewish community stands united, demonstrating that through unity and decisive action, they can uphold the values of tolerance, mutual respect, and social justice, ensuring the protection and well-being of Jewish individuals worldwide.

Chapter Five

Legal Safeguards:

Policy Measures Against Antisemitism

Introduction.

In an era where the resurgence of antisemitism is both alarming and pervasive, Australia's legislative and policy responses have been woefully inadequate. The critical shortcomings in Australia's approach underscore the urgency for sweeping reforms. Despite commendable bipartisan efforts, the existing legislative frameworks remain insufficient to combat the multifaceted threat posed by contemporary antisemitism. This chapter delves into the necessary legal protections and policy measures required to not only address hate crimes but also to fortify the societal values of safety, inclusivity, and justice.

The escalating frequency and severity of antisemitic incidents in Australia demand more than superficial legislative tweaks; they call for a comprehensive overhaul of the legal system to ensure that hate speech and hate crimes are met with the harshest possible penalties. Current laws have proven inadequate in deterring offenders or providing justice to victims.

Therefore, this chapter argues for the implementation of severe legal consequences, substantial fines, and extended prison sentences as vital deterrents. These legal measures must unequivocally convey that Australia will not tolerate any form of discrimination or violence against its citizens.

Moreover, educational programs and awareness campaigns are paramount in fostering a culture of empathy and understanding. Through education, the roots of hatred can be addressed, and future generations can be equipped to recognize and oppose antisemitism. Additionally, the critical role of law enforcement agencies and social media regulation in combating antisemitism is highlighted. Enhanced training for police officers, stringent oversight of online platforms, and robust community support systems are imperative to create a resilient and secure society.

This chapter is not merely a call to action but a demand for unwavering vigilance and decisive measures to eradicate antisemitism from the fabric of Australian society.

5.1 Legislative Frameworks: Strengthening Legal Protections Against Antisemitism.

In Australia, the legal framework addressing antisemitism is anchored in the International Holocaust Remembrance Alliance (IHRA) working definition of antisemitism. While not legally binding, this definition is instrumental for law enforcement agencies and social media companies in identifying and combating antisemitic incidents.

The IHRA definition covers both religious and racial forms of antisemitism, distinguishing legitimate criticism of Israel from antisemitism when it targets Jews as a group or Jewish individuals. Key legislative measures include the Racial Vilification Act 1989 and the Anti-Discrimination Act 1977 in New South Wales, prohibiting incitement to racial hatred and discrimination on grounds of race, religion, or ethnicity.

These laws have been effectively applied in various instances. For example, in 2023, Abdullah Al-Taay was charged for intimidating teenagers displaying an Israeli flag, with conditions imposed to prevent him from visiting areas where Jewish people congregate. This incident highlights proactive law enforcement against antisemitism.

Additionally, the denial of a visa to British conspiracy theorist David Icke in 2019, due to his antisemitic views, showcased the government's commitment to preventing hate speech. Dvir Abramovich of the ADC remarked, "This was a defining moment for who we are as a nation, and we salute the government for taking a clear-eyed and moral stance in rejecting hate and incitement."

However, the backlash Abramovich faced, marked by harassment and threats, underscores ongoing challenges. "This barrage of harassment, threats, and insults is chilling and unlike anything I have seen in recent times," he stated, yet affirmed the ADC's commitment to combatting hate.

The introduction of new legislative frameworks in Queensland marks a significant step towards addressing hate crimes and vilification. On March 29, 2023, Queensland enacted the Criminal Code (Serious Vilification and Hate Crimes) and Other Legislation Amendment Bill 2023, enhancing penalties for hate crimes and introducing offenses related to the public display of hate symbols. Premier Annastacia Palaszczuk asserted, "People armed with hate and prejudice and extreme ideologies won't be tolerated in Queensland," emphasizing the government's resolve.

Attorney-General Shannon Fentiman echoed this sentiment, emphasizing the gravity with which these reforms treat hate crimes. Community leaders like Christine Castley, CEO of Multicultural Australia, have welcomed these measures for improving safety for diverse communities.

In further efforts, Queensland introduced legislation on October 12, 2023, classifying serious vilification, including antisemitic chants, as a hate crime with penalties of up to three years' imprisonment. Rita Jabri Markwell from the Australian Muslim Advocacy Network highlighted that public expressions of hatred towards Jews would be considered hate crimes under the new laws.

Jason Steinberg from the Queensland Jewish Board of Deputies praised the legislation, emphasizing the deterrence of antisemitic behavior. Attorney-General Yvette D'Ath reiterated the commitment to eradicating serious vilification, stating that such actions have no place in society.

In New South Wales, the handling of a rally in Sydney on March 3, 2024, spotlighted challenges in managing hate speech and public order. During a pro-Palestine rally, antisemitic chants and the removal of a Jewish man with an Israeli flag escalated tension.

Despite the lack of charges, NSW Premier Chris Minns maintained, "Hate speech and racist language have no place in NSW," reflecting the state's firm stance against such behavior. This incident pointed to potential gaps in the existing legislative and enforcement frameworks.

In response to the rising threat of extremist symbols, Australia enacted significant measures in January 2024, criminalizing the Nazi salute and Nazi-related symbols, punishable by up to 12 months in prison. Attorney General Mark Dreyfus remarked, "This is the first legislation of its kind and will ensure no one in Australia will be allowed to glorify or profit from acts and symbols that celebrate the Nazis and their evil ideology."

The laws also ban the sale and trade of these symbols, aiming to eliminate financial benefits from hate-driven emblems. This action followed alarming incidents, such as antisemitic chants at a Sydney protest and Nazi salutes outside the Jewish Museum of Australia, underscoring the urgent need for legal intervention. Data from the Executive Council of Australian Jewry highlighted a spike in anti-Jewish incidents in late 2023, prompting these legislative efforts.

However, the implementation of these measures is just the beginning. Australia must adopt a zero-tolerance enforcement policy, enhance surveillance and intelligence capabilities, and mandate educational programs promoting tolerance to ensure the effectiveness of these laws. Law enforcement agencies should be empowered to act swiftly against violations using advanced technologies like high-definition cameras and social media monitoring tools.

Additionally, the legislative framework should be regularly reviewed and updated to address emerging threats, with international collaboration to share best practices in combating antisemitism and extremist ideologies. This multifaceted approach will fortify Australia's defenses against hate and terrorism, safeguarding inclusivity and respect for all citizens.

By April 29, 2024, Queensland had introduced stronger hate crime laws, increased penalties and criminalized the public display of hate symbols. These changes, moving serious vilification offenses to the Criminal Code, aim to streamline prosecution and provide harsher penalties, setting a precedent for other states.

Peter Wertheim of the Executive Council of Australian Jewry argued, "Current Federal criminal laws against racially motivated violence, incitement, and vilification have been shown to be unfit for purpose." Comprehensive and consistent legislation across all jurisdictions is critical to effectively address and deter hate crimes, promoting a safer society.

On May 27, 2024, Prime Minister Anthony Albanese announced plans to introduce new legislation criminalizing insults based on gender, sexuality, race, and religion, responding to rising incidents of antisemitism and Islamophobia. Attorney General Mark Dreyfus emphasized the government's commitment to shielding the community from extremism and violence.

This legislative push followed the vandalism of Mount Scopus Memorial College, intensifying calls for stronger legal protections. Jewish Labor MP Josh Burns and Victorian Liberal Senator Sarah Henderson condemned the incident, urging broader community efforts to combat antisemitism.

Attorney-General Mark Dreyfus is drafting hate speech laws to impose criminal penalties for serious vilification based on race, sexuality, gender, disability, or religion. The proposed legislation aims to strengthen federal protections, reflecting the government's view that existing laws are insufficiently enforced. The new hate speech bill is expected to enhance existing laws and create new criminal offenses for deliberate acts intended to incite violence or harm.

Bipartisan support for these initiatives underscores the shared recognition of the need to combat rising antisemitism and other forms of hate. Peter Wertheim criticized current federal criminal laws as inadequate, advocating for expanded legislation to address racially motivated violence and hate speech comprehensively.

In summary, the Australian government's legislative efforts represent a critical step towards strengthening legal protections for vulnerable communities. By addressing gaps in existing laws and ensuring hate crimes are met with appropriate legal consequences, these measures aim to create a safer and more inclusive society. The bipartisan support reinforces the commitment to protecting all Australians from hatred and extremism.

Given the escalating incidents of antisemitism, Australia must implement more robust measures to fortify its legislative frameworks against hate speech and hate crimes. While recent legislative developments represent a significant step forward, further enhancements are essential to ensure comprehensive protection for vulnerable communities. The following recommendations are not merely suggestions but urgent calls to action, demonstrating a zero-tolerance stance on antisemitism and all forms of hate.

First and foremost, harsher penalties for hate crimes and hate speech are critical. The deterrent effect of severe legal consequences cannot be overstated. Enhanced penalties, including substantial fines and extended prison sentences for offenders, will unequivocally signal that Australia will not tolerate discrimination or violence against any of its citizens.

Secondly, the role of education and awareness in combating antisemitism is paramount. Educational programs and awareness campaigns must be integrated into the national curriculum and extended to universities and the broader public. These initiatives should focus on fostering understanding and empathy, particularly among the youth, thereby empowering them to recognize and actively oppose hate speech and discrimination.

Furthermore, law enforcement agencies must be adequately trained to handle antisemitic incidents effectively. Comprehensive training on the International Holocaust Remembrance Alliance (IHRA) definition of antisemitism and its practical application is essential. This training will equip police officers to distinguish between legitimate criticism of Israel and antisemitism, ensuring that incidents are addressed appropriately and swiftly.

The regulation of social media platforms is another crucial area requiring stringent measures. Social media companies must be held accountable for moderating antisemitic content. Implementing stricter guidelines for reporting and removing hate speech, in collaboration with Jewish advocacy groups, is imperative to curb the proliferation of antisemitic behavior online.

Finally, strengthening community engagement and support for Jewish communities is vital in preventing antisemitic incidents. Increased funding for Jewish community centers, schools, and institutions, along with providing resources for individuals targeted by hate speech or violence, will bolster the resilience and security of these communities.

In conclusion, the proposed enhancements to Australia's legislative frameworks are not just beneficial but necessary. Harsher penalties, educational initiatives, enhanced law enforcement training, stringent social media regulation, and strengthened community support collectively form a robust defense against antisemitism. Australia must act decisively and aggressively to ensure that all forms of hate are met with the strongest possible legal repercussions, fostering a society where every individual is protected and respected.

5.2 Policy and Measures: Addressing Violent Protests and Public Disorder.

Recent violent protests targeting Jewish communities in Australia underscore a disturbing trend that demands comprehensive legal and law enforcement responses. One particularly alarming incident occurred during the Free Palestine Rally in Sydney, where pro-Palestinian protesters reportedly chanted antisemitic expletives. Similarly, there were distressing reports from Melbourne of Arabs 'hunting for Jews' and making direct threats against the Jewish community.

In Canberra, Jewish members of Parliament have stated that antisemitic incidents were 'off the charts' in Australia. The abuse includes threats of gun violence, threats to synagogues and to Jewish schools, as well as property damage and verbal abuse. Physical assaults have also been reported. These incidents highlight a pressing need for robust measures to ensure public safety and uphold the rule of law.

In response to these unsettling events, law enforcement agencies and community organizations have mobilized to address the violence and intimidation faced by Jewish communities. The Australian Jewish Association (AJA) has notably called on universities to take a firmer stance against vigilantism on campuses, characterized by pro-Palestinian groups aiming to intimidate and provoke conflict.

The Jewish Council of Australia has also condemned attacks on peaceful student-led Palestine solidarity encampments at universities, urging institutional leaders to safeguard democratic values and the right to free speech. These efforts reflect a concerted push to protect the safety and well-being of Jewish communities while preventing further acts of violence and intimidation.

Peter Wertheim, Co-CEO of the ECAJ, has been vocal about the inadequacies of current laws around hate speech and inciting violence. Wertheim pointed out that despite the introduction of Section 93Z of the Crimes Act in 2018, which was intended to curb such behavior, no charges or prosecutions have been initiated against those engaging in public displays of hate speech.

He highlighted an incident involving a neo-Nazi group in NSW and anti-Israel demonstrators at the Sydney Opera House, where chants such as 'Cull Kike' went unpunished.

"There is clearly a gap between what most people, and common sense, would regard as incitement to violence and the way the law defines it," Wertheim stated, underscoring the urgent need for legal reforms to better protect the public.

As discussed in Chapter One, the escalation of violent demonstrations following October 7 has witnessed Muslim communities taking the lead in large-scale protests, with the participation of white supremacists, academics, students, and Muslim radicals in their antisemitic actions. This has compelled some Jewish-owned businesses and residents in Melbourne's northern suburbs, including Northcote, Westgarth, and Thornbury, to relocate closer to Jewish community areas for safety. These dynamics underscore the profound impact of these violent protests on the social fabric and economic stability of Jewish communities.

The federal government's response has been marked by a disappointing lack of decisive action, according to many in the Jewish community. Despite having three Jewish Labor parliamentarians, including Attorney-General Mark Dreyfus, there is a sentiment that their efforts have fallen short.

Eliezer noted that Jewish Liberal Party politicians have similarly been ineffective in addressing these concerns. The Jewish community's growing disillusionment with Prime Minister Anthony Albanese and Foreign Minister Penny Wong's ability to curb antisemitic protests reflects a broader crisis of confidence in the government's commitment to their protection.

Law enforcement efforts have been reactive rather than preventive. For instance, during a planned pro-Palestine protest aimed at causing "economic pain" across Melbourne's CBD, police redeployed hundreds of officers from regional stations to manage the expected disruptions. This included specialist teams such as the mounted branch, public order response team, highway patrol, and transit police. Despite these measures, the police faced challenges in anticipating the locations and nature of the blockades, revealing gaps in intelligence and preparedness.

The violent confrontation at the Port of Melbourne, where pro-Palestinian demonstrators clashed with police and disrupted an Israeli delegation, further illustrates the volatile environment. The delegation, comprised of relatives of Israelis killed or abducted by terrorists, was forced to seek refuge in a police station after being harassed by protesters. This incident drew sharp condemnation from political leaders across the spectrum. Victoria state premier Jacinta Allan and opposition leader Peter Dutton both decried the behavior of the protesters, while Prime Minister Anthony Albanese denounced the actions as 'beyond contempt.'

These incidents highlight the urgent need for enhanced legislative frameworks and more proactive law enforcement strategies to address violent protests and public disorder targeting Jewish communities. Strengthening these measures is not only essential for the safety and security of Jewish Australians but also for the preservation of social harmony and democratic principles in the broader society.

A- Soft Preventive Measures.

Australia is facing an escalating threat of violent protests and public disorder, often driven by entrenched antisemitism and social unrest. To counteract these threats effectively, a comprehensive, preventive strategy is essential. This strategy must encompass rigorous policies focused on community engagement, unyielding dialogue, and robust conflict resolution initiatives. These measures are critical not only to deter violent actions but also to foster a resilient society capable of countering hate-driven unrest.

Community Engagement and Dialogue: The cornerstone of any preventive measure is robust community engagement and relentless dialogue. Establishing and maintaining strong relationships between law enforcement and the communities they serve is non-negotiable. The Australian Government's Community Engagement Strategy must be implemented with a zero-tolerance approach to any form of hesitation or delay. This strategy should include extensive community outreach programs, aggressive education initiatives, and collaborative efforts designed to tackle social and political issues decisively.

Intensive Community Outreach Programs: Programs aimed at fostering dialogue and understanding between different communities must be intensified. This includes mandatory participation in interfaith dialogues, cultural exchange events, and educational workshops designed to bridge gaps and reduce tensions.

Relentless Social Media Campaigns: Utilize social media platforms to promote messages of tolerance, respect, and unity aggressively, including Holocaust education. These campaigns should be continuous, with a clear, strong message that condemns antisemitism and any form of hate speech. This approach highlights the importance of educating people about the Holocaust to prevent similar atrocities in the future and to promote understanding and empathy towards the Jewish community.

Mandatory Community Forums: Regularly scheduled community forums and town hall meetings should be mandated, providing a platform for open dialogue and immediate redressal of community concerns. These forums must be facilitated by trained mediators to ensure productive and respectful exchanges.

Conflict Resolution Initiatives and Intensive Training Programs: Implementing conflict resolution initiatives is crucial in preventing violent protests. The Australian Centre for Conflict Resolution should be empowered to provide extensive mediation and negotiation services aimed at resolving disputes peacefully and decisively. Simultaneously, intensive training programs on conflict resolution and de-escalation techniques should be made mandatory for community leaders and activists, ensuring they are well-equipped to manage conflicts effectively and promote peaceful resolutions.

Enhanced Mediation and Conflict Management: Expand mediation services to ensure accessibility for all communities, including establishing centers in high-risk areas with 24/7 support. Develop proactive conflict management strategies that include early intervention, such as monitoring potential flashpoints and deploying mediation teams before conflicts escalate.

B- Hard Preventive Measures.

In addition to fostering community engagement and dialogue, it is imperative to implement harsh and robust measures to prevent violent protests and public disorder effectively. These measures must be designed to deter potential agitators and ensure a swift and decisive response to any signs of unrest.

Surveillance and Monitoring: Establish extensive surveillance and monitoring systems to identify and track potential agitators and instigators of violence. This includes the use of advanced technologies such as facial recognition software and predictive analytics to anticipate and prevent violent actions.

Strict Enforcement of Laws: Enforce laws related to hate speech, incitement to violence, and public disorder with uncompromising rigor. This includes imposing severe penalties for violations and ensuring swift prosecution of offenders.

Zero-Tolerance Policy: Implement a zero-tolerance policy towards any form of antisemitism or hate-driven actions. This policy should be communicated clearly and enforced consistently, leaving no room for ambiguity.

Intelligence Sharing: Facilitate robust intelligence sharing between law enforcement agencies, community organizations, and other stakeholders to ensure a coordinated and informed response to potential threats.

Emergency Response Teams: Establish and train emergency response teams capable of responding rapidly and effectively to violent protests and public disorder. These teams should be equipped with the necessary resources and authority to manage and de-escalate situations swiftly.

In summary, Australia must adopt a hardline stance against violent protests and ensure the safety of Jewish communities through a comprehensive and aggressive approach. This involves establishing rapid response units capable of efficiently managing violent protests, with officers receiving ongoing intensive training in crowd control, hate crime identification, and de-escalation techniques. These units should be equipped with advanced technology, such as surveillance drones, body cameras, and non-lethal weapons, to ensure swift action and effective evidence gathering.

Fortifying security at Jewish institutions is also essential, requiring increased police patrols, high-definition surveillance systems, secure entry points, and visible security personnel to deter potential attackers and ensure rapid response to any suspicious activity.

Additionally, law enforcement must undergo rigorous training to handle hate crimes effectively, learning to recognize and respond to antisemitic actions while mastering de-escalation and conflict resolution techniques. Building strong relationships between law enforcement, Jewish communities, and other affected groups through outreach programs, interfaith dialogues, and educational workshops is crucial for fostering understanding and reducing tensions.

Strengthening anti-protest laws is also necessary, including harsh penalties for physical violence, property damage, and incitement during protests, along with ensuring victims have access to legal recourse and protection. Reviewing and updating outdated legislation, such as the repealed Summary Offences and Sentencing Amendment Act in Victoria, is critical to providing adequate protection against violent protests.

The urgency of these measures is underscored by recent violent protests, such as the Free Palestine Rally in Sydney and the confrontations in Melbourne and Canberra, which have significantly impacted Jewish communities and public safety. The federal government must address the inadequacies in current hate speech and incitement laws, as highlighted by Peter Wertheim of the ECAJ, to protect Jewish Australians and uphold social harmony.

Therefore, a multifaceted approach that includes rigorous enforcement, legislative updates, and proactive community engagement is essential to effectively address violent protests and public disorder in Australia.

5.3 From Pulpits to Policy: Addressing the Trojan Horse of Antisemitism in Democratic Australia.

Following the October 7 attack by pro-Iranian militias on Israel, the narrative of Islamic antisemitism has undergone a significant shift. What was once characterized by sentiments of hatred and economic boycotts has escalated to include explicit calls for the eradication of Israel and the annihilation of Jewish communities worldwide, including those in Australia.

This intensification of antisemitic rhetoric highlights the broader impact of the ongoing conflict in the Middle East on Jewish communities globally, who now find themselves increasingly marginalized, persecuted, and under siege. This shift underscores the Islamization of the Gaza conflict and the broader Iranization of the Muslim struggle, often framed under the guise of liberating Al-Aqsa.

This intensified shift is exemplified by preachers like Kamal Abu Mariam and Abdul Salam Zoud. On November 24, 2023, Abu Mariam, in a Friday sermon at the Sydney Roselands Mosque, called for a boycott of any company supporting the "Zionist criminal apartheid Nazi Regime." He urged Muslims to emulate the Prophet Muhammad's attacks on enemy caravans and prayed for the destruction of the "plundering Jewish Zionists," stating further, "Count them, kill them one by one, and do not leave a single Jew alive."

Similarly, Imam Abdul Salam Zoud, in an antisemitic sermon at a Lakemba Mosque, labeled Jews as a "criminal, barbaric, tyrannical enemy" and advocated for jihad as the only solution 'for the sake of Allah.' Zoud asserted that jihad is the sole means for the restoration of Palestine and cited historical caliphates as examples of conquest through jihad.

Liberal Senator Dave Sharma condemned these sermons as 'disgusting' and 'un-Australian,' arguing that such rhetoric incites violence and should be unlawful. Peter Wertheim, Co-CEO of the Executive Council of Australian Jewry (ECAJ), emphasized the need for legal reforms to better address hate speech and incitement to violence. David Ossip, President of the NSW Jewish Board of Deputies, stressed that such hate-filled sermons undermine communal harmony and Australian values.

The Australian-Jewish community, represented by the ECAJ, is poised to take legal action against these preachers. ECAJ President Daniel Aghion called for stronger government action and legal protections against antisemitic hate speech. He criticized the lack of response from the Australian National Imams Council and other faith community leaders, highlighting the dangerous potential of unchecked hate speech to disrupt Australia's peaceful and cohesive society.

Federal Minister Tony Burke supported these calls for legal action and legislative measures, urging the government to strengthen existing laws. NSW Senator Dave Sharma also advocated for investigations and potential charges against the preachers, emphasizing the importance of political leaders defending against such hatred.

These hate preachers, occupying leadership roles in the Muslim community, exert significant influence over their audiences. Their messages are not merely seen as opinions but as authoritative legal rulings in accordance with Sharia law. Whether disseminated in mosques or through online platforms, their rhetoric has the potential to radicalize listeners, especially those already inclined towards extremism.

This radicalization can result in a dangerous redirection of anger from conflicts in the Middle East towards the local

Jewish community. This is particularly concerning given the presence of returning ISIS fighters, disillusioned Aboriginal youth, and white converts who may be susceptible to such messaging, as exemplified in cases such as the Cree Jihadist in Canada or Mark Taylor, also known as Jihadi John, in New Zealand.

These preachers, expanding their influence through various platforms, represent a Trojan Horse of antisemitism within democratic Australia, posing a continuous threat to its peaceful communities. Their advocacy for Jihad against Jews requires a nuanced examination, considering parallels with historical events like the Khaybar genocide or modern conflicts in the Levant.

This analysis is not merely an exercise in intellectual acrobatics; rather, it is crucial for understanding the Salafi Jihadi inclinations of these preachers. The plight of the exiled Yazidi community in Australia serves as a stark testament to the atrocities committed by individuals influenced by these ideologies, ranging from mass murder to enslavement and rape.

The concerning issue at hand is the apparent allowance for these Jihadi preachers to disseminate their antisemitic teachings in Australia over the span of decades, as discussed in Chapter Two. Their Salafi mosques, charities, and institutions have proliferated across the country, raising serious questions about the extent of their influence within Australian society.

This phenomenon underscores the urgent need for a critical examination of the regulatory frameworks governing religious institutions and the dissemination of extremist ideologies within democratic nations.

Recommendations.

As we have traversed through the ideological tapestry woven by Australian radical Imams, it becomes apparent that the 'Trojan Horse of Antisemitism' is more than a metaphor; it encapsulates the epistemic stealth through which antisemitic rhetoric infiltrates and corrodes democratic systems.

The escalating threat of Islamic radicalism and its deep-seated antisemitism demands robust and uncompromising measures, as recommended by the ECAJ and the ZFA. The spread of extremist ideologies facilitated by hate preachers represents a Trojan Horse within the democratic fabric of the nation, necessitating immediate and comprehensive action.

Firstly, stringent legislative measures are imperative. Enhanced surveillance of radical groups and individuals, including thorough monitoring of sermons and online activities of Imams, is crucial. Intelligence agencies must be equipped with the necessary tools and resources to track and prevent the dissemination of antisemitic rhetoric.

This surveillance must be complemented by de-radicalization programs aimed at providing alternative narratives and rehabilitative support to individuals susceptible to radical influences. Such programs should focus on promoting moderate and peaceful interpretations of Islam, countering the toxic ideologies propagated by hate preachers.

Financial oversight is paramount, requiring meticulous examination of funding sources and financial transactions linked to mosques, charities, and institutions suspected of promoting radical ideologies. This scrutiny encompasses both domestic and international funds that could fuel radical activities.

Disrupting the financial support to these extremist networks is essential to curtail their operational capabilities and influence. Illustrative instances include Hizb Ut-Tahrir Australia and Iranian associations, whose Imams are documented for disseminating antisemitic rhetoric, conspiracy theories, and holocaust denial, as elaborated in earlier sections.

Policy formulation must be inclusive, engaging academic experts, reformed radicals, and community leaders in developing effective countermeasures. This collaborative approach ensures a comprehensive understanding of the issues at hand and the creation of strategies that are both practical and impactful. The rapid spread of Islamic antisemitism and its proponents in Australia demands a nuanced and multifaceted response, integrating legal, social, and educational interventions.

De-platforming strategies should be employed to restrict the influence of individuals who actively propagate hate and radicalism. This includes removing their access to online platforms and public forums where they disseminate their toxic antisemitic ideologies. While this approach raises complex ethical considerations around freedom of speech, the protection of public safety and communal harmony must take precedence.

Visa policies warrant reassessment to bar the entry of foreign preachers with extremist inclinations. Stringent background checks and thorough assessments of ideological affiliations are imperative to prevent individuals posing a national security risk from entering the country. Visa cancellations and deportations, particularly of antisemitic Imams who are not Australian citizens, should be pursued to shield the nation from external extremist influences, a stance advocated by opposition leader Peter Dutton.

Moreover, tackling the underlying causes of religious antisemitism through community and interfaith initiatives is crucial. Encouraging open dialogues, fostering connections among diverse communities, and nurturing mutual understanding can mitigate the influence of radical ideologies and foster a more inclusive and tolerant society. Educational programs, interfaith forums, and collaborative projects involving religious and community leaders can significantly contribute to combating antisemitic rhetoric and violence while promoting social cohesion.

Additionally, Australian authorities should closely monitor Islamic institutions that propagate antisemitic rhetoric and incite jihad against Australian Jews. Institutions found to pose a threat to national safety and security should be promptly closed. For instance, the Ahlus Sunnah Wal Jamaah Association of Australia, based in Melbourne, has drawn scrutiny due to its connections with Jemaah Islamiyah and al-Qaeda. Similarly, institutions like the Lakemba Mosque in NSW and the Al-Madina Dawah Centre in Sydney should be subject to stringent oversight. Additionally, there should be rigorous monitoring and regulation of licenses for new institutions that exhibit inclinations towards jihadism and antisemitism in Australia.

Expanding on the issues raised in preceding chapters regarding the proliferation of online radicalization in Australia, the adoption of artificial intelligence (AI) technologies could represent a powerful tool for authorities. Models such as the EU 'Internet Referral Unit' could serve as a blueprint for Australian initiatives aimed at monitoring and scanning platforms like Telegram, Reddit, and specific message boards known for disseminating antisemitic content. To effectively combat such narratives, targeted social media campaigns should be crafted.

Collaborative efforts with major platforms such as Twitter and Facebook could be instrumental in launching 'counter-narrative' projects akin to Google 'Redirect Method.' This approach aims to steer individuals searching for extremist content towards material that challenges and refutes such ideologies. Integrating these technological strategies could bolster Australia's efforts to counter antisemitic propaganda and promote Holocaust education online.

In conclusion, Australian authorities and policymakers have long danced around the edges of the Trojan Horse of antisemitism, but the time for half-measures and blind spots has passed. The threat posed by radical ideologies is no longer theoretical; it is palpable, with pro-Palestinian protests escalating in both frequency and intensity, marked by a disturbing shift towards calls for the annihilation of Jews. This alarming trend underscores the urgent need for decisive action to protect national security and the safety of Jewish communities in Australia.

Addressing the **Trojan Horse of antisemitism** demands a comprehensive, multi-faceted approach. Legislative measures, including enhanced surveillance and de-radicalization programs, must be coupled with stringent financial oversight and targeted community initiatives. International collaboration is also crucial in combating the global spread of antisemitic rhetoric. Only through these robust and uncompromising strategies can Australia uphold its democratic values and shield its society from the insidious influence of violent antisemitism. The preservation of democratic integrity and national security hinges on unwavering vigilance and resolute action against those who seek to undermine them.

Chapter Five Conclusion.

This chapter underscores the dire need for Australian authorities to take decisive and uncompromising action against the rising tide of antisemitism. For far too long, policymakers have skirted around the edges of this Trojan Horse, allowing the threat to fester and grow. The recent surge in pro-Palestinian protests, marked by increasingly aggressive and violent rhetoric, including calls for the annihilation of Jews, highlights the urgency of addressing this issue head-on. The safety of Jewish communities and the integrity of Australia's democratic values are at stake, and robust measures must be implemented without delay to ensure national security and social harmony.

A multifaceted approach is imperative to combat the multifarious nature of antisemitism. Legislative frameworks must be fortified to ensure that hate speech and hate crimes are met with severe penalties, serving as a powerful deterrent against such acts. Comprehensive education and awareness programs must be integrated into the national curriculum to foster understanding and empathy from a young age. Additionally, law enforcement agencies need specialized training to effectively handle antisemitic incidents, equipped with the knowledge to differentiate between legitimate criticism and hate speech.

Social media platforms must also be held accountable for moderating and removing antisemitic content, working in close collaboration with Jewish advocacy groups to curb the spread of hate online. Furthermore, strengthening community engagement and providing robust support for Jewish communities will enhance their resilience and security.

The escalating frequency and intensity of violent protests, such as the Free Palestine Rally in Sydney, further underscore the critical need for a hardline stance against public disorder and antisemitism. Rapid response units, advanced surveillance technology, and fortified security at Jewish institutions are essential components of an effective strategy. Law enforcement must build strong relationships with Jewish communities and other affected groups to foster mutual understanding and reduce tensions.

Updating outdated legislation and enforcing anti-protest laws with severe penalties for incitement and violence are crucial steps in maintaining public order and protecting vulnerable communities. In conclusion, Australia's commitment to combating antisemitism must be unwavering, marked by rigorous enforcement, comprehensive legislative updates, and proactive community engagement. Only through such resolute and aggressive measures can Australia safeguard its democratic values and ensure the safety and dignity of all its citizens.

Book Conclusion

The discourse surrounding antisemitism in Australia reveals a landscape fraught with complexity and urgency. The resurgence of antisemitism, intensified by global conflicts and local dynamics, demands an unwavering and comprehensive response. The multifaceted nature of antisemitism and its dire consequences on individuals and communities underscore the necessity of a strategic, multifaceted approach to combat this persistent threat.

The alarming resurgence of antisemitism across the nation has a profound impact on the Jewish community and broader society. Education, legal reforms, and community engagement are crucial in addressing this deep-seated prejudice. The urgent call for collective action emphasizes the necessity of preserving Australia's values of diversity and inclusivity, ensuring a harmonious and respectful multicultural society.

The interconnectedness of global and local antisemitism is evident, as conflicts abroad exacerbate antisemitism worldwide, including in Australia, where Jewish communities face heightened discrimination and violence. The need for robust measures to protect and support Jewish communities is paramount, highlighting the interconnected nature of global Jewish security and the stability of the Middle East.

Balancing the fight against antisemitism with the preservation of free expression and academic freedom is a delicate task. Nuanced approaches and ongoing dialogue are necessary to ensure that efforts to combat antisemitism do not inadvertently undermine other essential freedoms. The pivotal role of Jewish organizations and political leaders in defining and addressing antisemitism is crucial for effective action.

Jewish solidarity plays a critical role in combating antisemitic rhetoric and violence. The collective efforts of Jewish organizations and leaders demonstrate the power of unified action. Legal frameworks, educational campaigns, and strategic collaborations foster a resilient and cohesive Jewish community, essential for addressing antisemitism effectively.

Decisive and uncompromising action from Australian authorities is imperative. Fortifying legislative frameworks, integrating comprehensive education programs, and enhancing law enforcement capabilities are essential steps in combating antisemitism. Addressing violent protests and public disorder requires robust security measures and severe penalties for hate crimes and incitement.

However, the landscape of antisemitism is far from uniform; it presents itself in various shades and forms, often tailored to the specific dynamics of each community. This diversity makes combating antisemitic rhetoric a complex and challenging task. Addressing this issue is akin to unraveling a **Gordian knot**: a complex tangle of interconnected challenges, each reinforcing the others.

This complexity requires a multifaceted approach to effectively counter this deep-rooted prejudice. Dealing with antisemitism in Australia demands more than a singular solution; it necessitates a combination of both robust and nuanced measures.

Untangling the Gordian knot symbolizes the dichotomy yet interconnectedness of intervention methods. Hard measures, such as legislation, the de-platforming of hate preachers, and enhanced surveillance, focus on immediate containment, akin to cutting through the knot. Conversely, soft measures, including community engagement, cognitive reform, Holocaust education, and the promotion of moderate religious leaders, aim to unravel the knot thread by thread, offering a more sustainable but gradual solution. Both approaches are essential for a comprehensive strategy against the pervasive Trojan Horse of antisemitism.

In conclusion, combating antisemitism in Australia necessitates a relentless and comprehensive strategy that combines legal enforcement, educational initiatives, and community solidarity. The resilience and determination of the Jewish community, supported by robust policy frameworks and international collaboration, are critical in addressing the multifaceted challenges posed by antisemitism. Through unity and decisive action, Australia can uphold the values of tolerance, mutual respect, and social justice, ensuring the protection and well-being of its Jewish citizens and fostering a society that stands resilient against hate in all its forms.

References

Abascal, D. (2023). Iran counts on the Polisario Front in its global terrorist network against Israel and Morocco. ATALAYAR (November 11, 2023).

ADL (April 16, 2024). Massive spike post-Oct. 7 recorded; campus incidents tripled; bomb threats targeting Jewish institutions up 10 times.

AJN Staff (2024). Another cleric delivers antisemitic sermon. Australian Jewish News (March 14, 2024).

Amy, R. (2024). Scott Morrison accuses UN of antisemitism and applying double standards against Israel. The Guardian (February 19, 2024).

Avrahami, Z. (2024). 'Sinwar, we will not let you die,' protesters chant in Malmo. Yedioth Ahronoth (May 9, 2024).

Avrahami, Z. (2024). 'Their songs call for the rape of Jewish women,' Israeli student in Geneva says. Yedioth Ahronoth (May 10, 2024).

Begley, P. (2024). Morrison accuses UN of antisemitism, decries 'persecution' of Australian Jews. Sydney Morning Herald (February 18, 2024).

Betts, A. (2024). What to Know About the Campus Protests Over the Israel-Hamas War. The New York Times (April 20, 2024).

Bolt, A. (2023). 'Fired up' hate preacher in Australia calls for jihad in 'frightening' footage. Sky News Australia (November 6, 2023).

Bramston, T. (2023). History shows where snowballing hatred can lead. The Hamas barbarism of October 7 demonstrates Israel will remain imperiled as long as Hamas has control of Gaza. The Australian (November 15, 2023).

Butler, J. (2023). Peter Dutton accused of 'weaponizing antisemitism' during fiery debate in parliament. The Guardian (November 15, 2023).

Canales, S. B. (2024). 'Tone deaf': Port Arthur survivor criticizes Peter Dutton's comparison of pro-Palestine protest to massacre. The Guardian (April 12, 2024).

Cashman, G. F. (2024). Antisemitism in Australia isn't a simple problem to fix. The Jerusalem Post (March 1, 2024).

Caulcutt, C. (2023). French Jews live in fear amid rising antisemitism following Hamas attacks. Politico (October 30, 2023).

Charles, B. (2024). Australia's pro-Palestinian activists to continue targeting Israeli ships. Al-Jazeera (January 29, 2024).

Cheshire, T. (2024). Rival Gaza protests in London seethed with mutual animosity - providing visceral evidence of deep and angry divides. Sky News (March 31, 2024).

Clench, S. (2018). 'What a joke': Parliament erupts after controversial accusation. Sydney News (October 18, 2018).

Collins, P. (2024). Ex-prime ministers Scott Morrison and Tony Abbott lead uproar against Australia's vote to admit Palestine to the UN, claiming the move 'rewards terrorists'. Daily Mail Australia (May 11, 2024).

Coote, J. (2023). Pro-Palestinian rally at Lakemba in Sydney criticized for 'celebration' of attacks on Israel. ABC News (October 9, 2023).

Credlin, P. (2023). 'Vile': More evidence emerges of 'rank anti-Semitism' in Sydney Mosque. Sky News Australia (November 07, 2023).

Doherty, L. (2021). Australian government to adopt international group's definition of antisemitism. The Guardian (October 15, 2021).

Economist, The. (November 9, 2023). Antisemitism surges in France after the Hamas attacks on Israel.

Edelman, S. (2024). Antisemitic teens terrorizing Jewish teacher with Hitler jabs, death threats as NYC school refuses to discipline them: 'I live in fear'. New York Post (March 2, 2024).

Elukin, J. (2020). Antisemitism: Understanding and Teaching the Holocaust. https://doi.org/10.2307/j.ctv11hps49.5.

Frost, N. (2023). Antisemitic and Islamophobic Incidents Surge in Australia. Tensions between religious groups in Australia have risen since the start of the Israel-Hamas war. The New York Times (November 6, 2023).

Furlan, M. (2022). Israeli-Iranian relations: past friendship, current hostility. Taylor & Francis Online (February 18, 2022).

Ganko, J. (2024). Young children chant anti-Israel slogans at Sydney university protest. Sydney Morning Herald (April 29, 2024).

Gavlak, D. (2024). Analysts: Iran Using Gaza War to Consolidate Regional Influence. Voice of America (March 04, 2024).

Goldin, M. (2024). Antisemitism Down Under Is Turning Vicious. Newsweek (February 06, 2024).

Guterres, A. (2018). The Power of Education for Countering Racism and Discrimination: The Case of anti-Semitism. United Nations Adress (September 26, 2018).

Harel, A. (2024). Hezbollah Has Harmed Israel's North with Far More Than Rockets, as Escalation Brews. Haaretz (February 15, 2024).

Harris, R. (2021). Australia to back international definition of anti-Semitism. Sydney Morning Herald (October 14, 2021).

Hassan, A. M. (2024). Canadian man shot dead in Egypt among rising tensions. Independent (May 08, 2024).

Hirsh, D. (2007). Anti-Zionism and Antisemitism: Cosmopolitan Reflections. Department of Sociology, Goldsmiths, University of London.

Hoffman, G. et Al. (2023). New Australian PM 'very critical' of Israel. The Jerusalem Post (May 23, 2022).

Holt, F. (2024). 300 Jews Walk child to school after he faced antisemitic bullying. Jewish Chronicle (May 21, 2024).

Houston, C. & McMillan, A. (2024). Police redeploy officers to quell potential chaos from pro-Palestine blockades. The Age (April 14, 2024).

Hyams, J. (2023). Why we need the IHRA definition of antisemitism. AIJAC (March 17, 2023).

Jewish Chronicle (APRIL 09, 2024). Gaza civilians sold me to Hamas, says former hostage. Jewish News Syndicate (2024).

Jikeli, G (2020). Is Religion Coming Back as a Source for Antisemitic Views? College of Arts and Sciences, Indiana University, Bloomington (May 20, 2022).

Kantor, K. (2018). Antisemitism Worldwide. Moshe Kantor Database for the Study of Contemporary Antisemitism and Racism. European Jewish Congress.

Karp, P. (2023). When Peter Dutton claims Labor isn't horrified enough about Hamas, it doesn't help anyone. The Guardian (October 11, 2023).

Kelsall, T. (2022). Upper House recognizes antisemitism definition. In-Daily (July 08, 2022).

Khalil, A. (2024). Pro-Palestinian protesters rally in Washington to mark a painful present and past. Los Angeles Times (May 18, 2024).

Lapin, A. (2023). Antisemitism reportedly spikes and US Jews face violent threats amid climate of fear over Israel-Hamas war. Jewish News of Northern California (October 24, 2023).

Lauder, R. S. (2019). WJC President Ronald S. Lauder calls for unity in fight against hate in address to Vatican officials. World Jewish Congress (November 8, 2019).

Laurence, K. (2024). This is not normal: Anti-Defamation Commission chairman Dvir Abramovich says Jews have 'had enough' of 'out of control' anti-Semitism. Sky News (May 27, 2024).

Lyons, E. (2024). Australia bans Nazi salute, swastika, other hate symbols in public as antisemitism spikes. CBS News (January 8, 2024).

MacDonald, T. (2023). 'Deeply disturbing': Montreal police investigating two firebombing at Jewish institutions. Global News (November 7, 2023).

Maltz, J. (2024). Six Months On: How October 7 and the Gaza War Transformed Jews Across the Globe. Haaretz (April 7, 2024).

Margolis, D. (2001). The Muslim Zionist. Los Angeles Jewish Journal (February 23, 2001).

Marin, S. (2024). for The Religion and Ethics Report (February 14, 2024).

Marks, J. (2024). Journalist, doctor held Israelis hostage in Gaza. Pittsburg Jewish Chronicle (June 9, 2024).

Marsh, S. & Rinke, A. (2023). Germany's Scholz 'ashamed' at antisemitism wave as 'Kristallnacht' pogrom marked. Reuters (November 9, 2023).

Media Release (2021). Waverley Council adopts International Holocaust Remembrance Alliance working definition of antisemitism. Waverly Council (November 19, 2021).

MEM (2024). Israel: TV channel claims Al-Azhar curriculum 'incites hatred'. Middle East Monitor (February 1, 2024).

Mercer, P. (2023). Australian Pro-Palestinian Protesters Storm Israeli Delegation Hotel Lobby. Voice of America (December 01, 2023).

Middleton, K. (2024). Rhetoric with no policy, vision with no detail: Dutton and Albanese have big gaps to fill. The Guardian (April 12, 2024).

Milienos, A. (2024). Sydney imam gives a shocking anti-Semitic sermon at Masjid As-Sunnah Mosque in Lakemba. Daily Mail Australia (March 10, 2024).

Morrow, J. (2023). Bipartisan fury over 'kill the Jew' sermon. The Daily Telegraph (November 7, 2023).

Nahal, T. (2019). Elan Carr named new U.S. envoy to fight anti-Semitism. Politico (February 5, 2019).

Nathan, J. (2019). Report on Antisemitism in Australia 2019. Executive Council of Australian Jewry. (October 1, 2018 – September 30, 2019).

O'Connor, T. (2023). Not Only Hamas: Eight Factions at War with Israel in Gaza. Newsweek (November 08, 2023).

Perry, S. (2024). Saudi authorities forbid speaking out against normalization with Israel. Yedioth Ahronoth (April 5, 2024).

Ransley, A. (2023). Anthony Albanese, Penny Wong's response to attack on Israel draws criticism. The Australian (October 08, 2023).

Ransley, A. (2023). Anthony Albanese, Penny Wong's response to attack on Israel draws criticism. The Australian (October 08, 2023).

Reuters (2023). Two Israelis, one Egyptian shot dead in Alexandria, Israeli foreign ministry says. Reuters, Middle East (October 8, 2023).

Reuters (May 14, 2024). Two men in UK court accused of machine gun plot to kill Jewish people.

Reyes, R. (2024). Publicly funded arts center cancels Jewish school's event over Gaza 'genocide'. New York Post (June 16, 2024).

Romero, D. et Al. (2024). Columbia to hold classes virtually as Jewish leaders warn of safety amid tensions over pro-Palestinian protests. NBC News (April 22, 2024).

Rutland, S. (2023). The long, dark history of antisemitism in Australia. The Conversation (November 23, 2023).

Sallon, H. (2023). Iran's latent front in Syria poses a real threat to Israel. Le Monde (October 28, 2023).

Salt, J. (2024). Hypocrisy and Deceit Down Under – Is Australia a Zionist Stronghold? Palestine Chronicle (May 31, 2024).

Schaer, C. (2023). Israel-Hamas war: What role do Iran-backed militias play? DW (October 24, 2023).

Silva, K. (2024). Human rights activist charged over alleged kidnapping and assault of a man in Melbourne. ABC News (March 12, 2024).

Singh, K. (2023). Trudeau says Canada faces 'scary rise' in antisemitism after war in Middle East. Reuters (October 18, 2023).

Staff, TOI (2024). Columbia protest leader banned from campus for saying 'Zionists don't deserve to live'. The Times of Israel (April 27, 2024).

Staff, TOI. (2024). Hamas wish list of prisoners includes terror masterminds of Second Intifada. The Times of Israel (February 5, 2024).

Tillet, A. (2018). Scott Morrison calls in cops after ASIO leak warning over Israel embassy move. Financial Review (Oct 18, 2018).

Times of Israel (March 10, 2023). Netanyahu to German paper: Arab leaders publicly condemn Israel but privately back war against Hamas.

TOI (2024). 'Kill another Zionist now': Pro-terror demonstrators converge near White House. Times of Israel (June 8, 2024).

TRT World (2023). Australians prevent Israeli cargo ship from docking at Sydney port. (November 11, 2023).

Warrick, J. et Al. (2023). Not Only Hamas: Eight Factions at War with Israel at Gaza. The Washington Post (November 8, 2023).

Webman, E. (2019). Redeeming Humanity from the Evil of the Jews: Islamist Rationalization of Antisemitism. Comprehending and Confronting Antisemitism. https://doi.org/10.1515/9783110618594-019.

Weiss, B. (2019). How to Fight Anti-Semitism. Crown Publisher (September 10, 2019).

Wistrich, R. S. (2017). Antisemitism in the Age of Jewish Empowerment. University of Nebraska Press.

About the Author

Hamid Fernana Hails from the Sahara Region of Morocco and served as a Community Leader in South Africa for 20 Years. He has spent 9 Years as a Research Fellow at the University of Free State, Bloemfontein, South Africa.

* 9 7 9 8 2 2 4 6 6 0 9 5 7 *